WORKING WITH VOLUNTEERS

SKILLS FOR LEADERSHIP

EMILY KITTLE MORRISON

FISHER BOOKS

Publishers: Helen V. Fisher
              Howard W. Fisher
              Fred W. Fisher

Art Director: Josh Young

Published by Fisher Books
PO Box 38040
Tucson, Arizona 85740-8040
(602) 292-9080

**Library of Congress
Cataloging-in-Publication Data**

Morrison, Emily K. (Emily Kittle)
    Working with volunteers.

    Reprint. Previously published:
    Skills for leadership.
    Bibliography: p.
    Includes index.
    1. Voluntarism.
    2. Volunteers—training of.
    3. Leadership. I. title.
HN49.V64M67 1988 361.3'7
    88-24412
ISBN 1-55561-015-3 (pbk.)

Printed in United States of America
Printing 10 9 8 7 6 5 4 3

Fisher Books are available at special
quantity discounts for educational
use. Special books, or book excerpts,
can also be created to fit specific
needs. For details please write or
telephone.

ACKNOWLEDGEMENTS

My first word of thanks go to my family for enduring the months of research and writing that went into this book, then to my editorial assistants Libby Kittle and Amanda Harries. I thank them for their hours, their insights and their expertise in helping me bring this to its final form. In addition to hours of typing, Linda Waldrop was invaluable to me, bringing a new perspective to my work. For this I thank her. And, to Ann Bannard, a special thanks for her hours and interest in helping to proof this second edition.

Besides these, I am indebted to many bright and creative trainers with whom I have worked. Karen Meyer, Carol Torrey, Marty Squire, Martha Hunter, Kathleen Henze, Charline Franz, Susan Rose, Anne Gould, Shannon Rosenblatt, Barbara Henward, Mary Ell Ruffner, Sally Schaefer, Susan Shultz, Ileen Lashinsky, and Nan Kozdruy.

CONTENTS

HOW TO USE THIS BOOK

All the information, check lists and guidelines included in this book are presented for your use. It is my hope that you will adapt, edit, reproduce and recreate those materials that appear pertinent to your organization.

These forms and key concepts can be included in a Board Orientation packet, used as handouts in skill workshops or adapted as worksheets for sessions designed to facilitate discussion, to problem solve, or to establish new direction.

Highlights and specific points can be used graphically on flip charts or transparencies as visual aids in training sessions with staff, Boards, and volunteers.

It is *not* necessary to request specific permission to use these material for any non-profit endeavor. However, a note of credit to the source may prove useful later on, and would be considerate to my contributors.

Introduction

Not long ago I found myself saying, "Most of what I know about working with people I've learned in the last 5 years!" The regrettable thing is that the information would have been so useful to me in the early years of my volunteer life — it would have helped me to invest my time more wisely, more productively, and would have provided me with a great many more successes and fewer frustrations.

Often we don't realize we need specific information to be successful volunteers. After all, "We're *just* volunteers." Right? Wrong! We are not JUST anything — least of all, volunteers. Each hour we give represents many saved by a community that would otherwise be left without the service, or in a position of taxing to provide salaried personnel to do the job.

And not JUST a volunteer, because if we plan carefully, we, too, are gaining from this involvement in the community. We are gaining numerous skills, considerable experience, and possibly contacts, and this is over and above the feelings of pride and self worth gained from contributing to the betterment of the community.

Library shelves are filled with volumes with such titles as *Creative Use of Volunteers, Developing your Volunteer Community, Volunteer Training and Development, Working with Volunteers*, and the list goes on. These are all useful to those supervising volunteers, but what about the volunteer himself? I've been a volunteer, active in my community, for 30 years. The last few have been devoted to training. Only in these last years have I been aware of the many resources available to help volunteers function more effectively. It's the answer sheet the teacher had — and we the students never even knew the questions to ask.

What I hope to do is share with you, in a compact handbook, many of the tricks of the trade I've come upon through experience, through research and through interviews. This revision of my first book, *"How to Get the Most Out of Being a Volunteer,"* includes updated material as well as additions which I feel will add to its usefulness.

I have divided the information, with the idea that you can consult a pertinent chapter when the material is of immediate use to you. You cannot expect to find all the answers. Nor are these the *only* answers. These are concepts that have worked for me. I want to share them with you. I have spent the past 10 years training other volunteers in leadership skills. Much of the material contained within has come from these workshops. I've tried to be as brief as possible, but my background material has been considerable. I encourage you to explore further any topic of interest to you. For this I have included a reference section.

"People get out of life exactly what they put into it." Most volunteers have figured this out. We get so much by giving to others. That is our real motivation for remaining involved.

The sad part is when interpersonal relations create frustration and disappointment. Many of these problems can be nipped in the bud or avoided totally. That is what this book is all about. Within these chapters you will find skills for leadership which will help you to get the most out of being a volunteer.

This handbook is by no means all-inclusive, nor should it be considered original. Contained within these pages are tools for success. To what extent you will find them useful, or even agree with them, will depend on your background and perspective. These are things that have worked for me as a "Perpetual Volunteer."

1. Volunteers

"Get Your Good Feelings"

There are some things that belong to us that are so precious we can't sell them; we must share them with others — so it is with our volunteer efforts.

> "What I spent, is gone
> what I kept, is lost
> but what I gave to charity
> will be mine forever"
> Epitaph

There is a certain reward in being a part of an effort that makes a difference. In contemporary society the problems are complex, the solutions more involved, and the satisfactions more obscure. It is these very challenges which spark the interest and involvement of 20th century volunteers. This involvement meets inner needs and brings happiness.

> "Happiness is the utilization of one's talents along
> lines of excellence"   Aristotle

TRENDS IN VOLUNTARISM

Today a far greater percentage of the population is involved in volunteer efforts then at any time in history. A new consciousness of domestic deprivation, the beginning of racial militancy and rising affluence (permitting increased leisure), have all affected voluntarism.

Many customary recipients of volunteer services are now serving their own community — the young, the old, the handicapped, and the poor. Voluntarism now includes every economic group — no more "Lady Bountiful".

PERIODS OF TRANSITION

Four transition periods brought us where we are today in American voluntarism. The first was Colonization. Voluntarism was necessary for survival. Church work, town councils and barn raisings are examples.

The second was the Civil War (until the 30's.) Voluntarism changed from individual charity to organized programs (Red Cross, YWCA, Hull House, Salvation Army, Boy Scouts, Goodwill, etc.). World War I saw the beginning of domestic issues and the establishment of the American Hearing Society, Crippled Children Society, Foundation for the Blind, for example. The Depression brought local relief activities: Community Chest, charities and service became Big Business.

The third was a change from an upper class activity to that of the middle class: the establishment of March of Dimes, and other nickel and dime collections, and such things as pay roll deductions. World War II brought staggering growth: health and welfare organizations and door to door fund raising began in earnest.

Finally the fourth: Participatory Democracy. Voluntarism began to represent all segments of society and with it came the birth of self-help groups.

OVERVIEW

The tradition of volunteering evolved not just from altruism but a combination of religious spirit (of man's humanity to man) and a dose of mutual dependence and assistance.

"To portray our history as though it were related solely to goodness of heart may describe the best in our forefathers, but would not identify the widespread tradition of organized neighborliness which hardship dictated and goodness tempered."

Brian O'Connell (Effective Leadership in
Voluntary Organizations)

We must be pleased that so many people are concerned enough to express their caring, and that our freedoms continue to provide these opportunities. Today, anyone who cares and is prepared to do something about that caring can make a difference. But, many need training in how to make things happen, and more and more organizations are recognizing the importance of making this training available.

An 'Action Orientation' was the focus of the 50's. The current thrust is toward 'Advocacy', speaking up for causes and concerns — lobbying. However, most voluntary organizations spend considerable time and effort 'doing'. For effectiveness and efficiency, groups would be wise to recognize the importance of needs assessment, training and evaluation. I have a strong bias for the investment in on-going skill development and assessment of current effectiveness in meeting needs and objectives.

Nothing is constant but change itself. Because of this a consciousness must be raised in our volunteer leaders to the ever changing needs of our constituents, clients *and* volunteers.

Beyond these more immediate concerns, there are broad based concerns for the future. These include:

1. State and local ordinances which limit organization's ability to function

2. Tax exemption restrictions

3. IRS accounting (which can be confusing)

4. Too much conservatism

5. Congressional proposals which could limit activities (such as student activism)

6. Federal restrictions on public interest law firms

7. Tax laws which discourage charitable giving

In a country based on the belief in freedom, government should be involved (in voluntarism) only to the extent that it preserves the rights and freedoms which allow activities to flourish.

More and more efforts are being exercised to form coalitions and to begin to "network" with other organizations and agencies in an attempt to avoid the duplication of time, money and manpower. The National Center for Citizen Involvement is a fine example (on a national scale) of sharing ideas and resources. Locally, in communities all across the country, groups are beginning to work together to bring about change. They are sharing office space, phone lines, address lists, manpower, and expertise.

FOCUS ON VOLUNTARISM

Who Volunteers And Why?

A WIDER VARIETY OF PEOPLE THAN EVER BEFORE:

- UNEMPLOYED, MIDDLE CLASS WOMEN — probably always will, to demonstrate a commitment to their community, to advance causes they care about, and for purely social reasons
- EMPLOYED AND PROFESSIONAL PEOPLE — always have, to challenge talents and skills untapped on the job . . . and it's "good business"
- RETIRED PEOPLE — more than ever. We are a healthier nation and our senior citizens are filled with ability, interest and life . . . volunteering allows them to continue to feel needed (which they are!)
- TEENAGERS — to gain a sense of self worth, to develop skills, and to demonstrate their dependability and initiative (supervisors are great references for real jobs) . . . and many volunteer jobs lead to paid jobs, if just through "contacts"
- THE UNEMPLOYED — to make these same kinds of contacts, as a form of career development, and to diminish the negative feelings which accompany the state of unemployment
- THE NEEDY — more and more self-help groups are springing up within communities and sub-groups, whether neighborhoods needing improvement or individuals with MS working to raise funds for MS research
- PRESCHOOLERS — Some Veterans' Hospitals have Moppet Programs which train and involve little people in activities in the Geriatric Ward. It's good for everyone
- NEWCOMERS — to make friends and to become involved in their new communities . . . usually associating with an organization which interested them back home

What Are The Effects Of Economic Policies On Voluntarism?

- Presidential belief in the potential of volunteers has been significant in raising the consciousness of the country to the possibility of making a difference through voluntary action. This has given the volunteer some prestige. It's hard to look down on a whole segment of the population which the President has praised . . .

- Because of Federal cutbacks there will be a greater need than ever to provide services which have come to be expected ... which were formerly provided by the government.

- Because of budget cuts agencies and organizations are going to have to fill in for dollars which government previously provided to assist in their programs ...

- Services, as well as money support, are being reduced ... it will take a volunteer commitment to continue the activities — from research to hot meals. The "Philosophy of Entitlement" has raised a generation to "expect" that someone (else) will provide them with many things in their lives ...

- There will be many more advocacy efforts ... individuals and groups speaking out for causes and changes they believe in ...

- The dollar value of volunteer time in 1980 was over 64 billion, and this is apt to go up ... whereas the combined money contribution of individuals, corporations, and foundations, which was nearly 48 billion (according to a study by The Independent Sector) is likely to go down as inflation cuts into our discretionary income, and tax laws discourage contributions ...

- 52% of all Americans over 13 (according to Gallup) volunteer in some manner ... 84 million are associated with structured programs such as Scouting and Red Cross. The higher the education level the higher the number of hours (as well as dollars) donated ... time donated will continue at about the same level, though the mix of who is volunteering is changing ...

What Can Organizations Do To assure Leadership For The Future?

- First, and primarily, organizations must recognize the need for continuing education ... in part because of perpetual changes (particularly in personnel, which we must expect in any nonprofit organization), and in part because each new experience we have in life makes us receptive to different things.

- Assure effectiveness, and leadership. Recognize that an orientation should be presented annually ... even if the manpower or Board happens to remain basically the same (which is very unlikely) ... the situation and direction change. Those responsible for these changes should have a chance to clarify their expectations and understand the expectations of workers.

- Focus as much attention on the "process" and the people as we are typically giving to the "task." We need to recognize the potential of new volunteers, and to provide avenues for development . . . to allow for committee assignments, then co-chairmanships, then chairmanships and Board positions. (This experience helps build Leadership).

- Part of Leadership comes from a confidence level felt within (because we feel a part of a group, and we feel capable of handling the situations and the people) . . . a conscious effort should be made to develop a sense of team within the group, and to learn about people as talented individuals beyond their role in the group.

- Interaction meetings allow members of the group to feel they are truly a part of things and their feelings are heard. In terms of Leadership development — the task of "facilitator" can be rotated so each member has a chance to lead. (These meetings depend on a planned agenda, a flip chart and broad pens for recording and tape so each completed sheet of notes can be posted for all to see). See chapter 2 on meetings.

- A good entrance interview and wise placement can put you in touch with the abilities of the volunteers. A periodic "needs assessment" will keep you current as to the motivation and areas of interest of each member, so he can be challenged and his retention better assured. Skill banks are wonderful tools for staying on top of where the talent is, and knowing where to go when your organization has specific needs.

- Expecting that those around you "bring solutions not problems" to your attention allows members to develop skills within themselves rather than looking for answers in others.

- A policy which discourages members from serving more than 2 consecutive years on a Board will challenge you to look for new people. Typically Board members are the group's happiest . . . increase the percentage of members with Board experience.

Are There Resources In The Community To Help Agencies And Organizations In Training Their Volunteers?

- Local and National leadership development trainers offer training sessions periodically to the public, as well as workshops designed for specific groups, to deal with their personnel and specific interests. The American Society for Training and Development, is composed of individuals working in the Human Resources Development field, and though primarily professionals with major corporations, it is possible to get assistance through this organization.

- National Speakers Association is made up of many talented individuals prepared to address organization on a wide range of topics, beginning with Motivation.

- The association of Junior Leagues has as its purpose: To demonstrate the effectiveness of trained volunteers ... and to this end they often have among their services to the community a program which provides trainers to come to an organization and work with it. Many offer specific workshops, such as Management By Objectives.

- Organizations such as United Way, Girl Scouts, the Y, Red Cross and others have long realized the need for, and believed in, training. I would like to see more cooperation among agencies to share experts, and to open training sessions to others.

- University Associates of La Jolla, California, produce wonderful manuals for training which can serve as guides to organizations interested in developing their own training resources.

- Associations such as Volunteer, DOVIA (Directors of Volunteers in Agencies) and the Association of Volunteer Directors are all helpful resources devoted to voluntarism.

- The library is filled with material from management to motivation and though much is designed for business, the concepts are quite transferable to the volunteer setting.

- My own book, *How to Get the Most out of Being a Volunteer* is a handbook of checklists and guidelines, filled with key concepts for consideration. Other such books are available through the National Center for Citizen Involvement in Arlington, Virginia.

**What About Staff? Do They Need Training In
How To Deal Effectively With Volunteers?**

- All of your efforts in recruiting, orienting and training can be for naught if the volunteer must work with a staff person who views him as an aggravation.

- The staff should be shown just how volunteers agument the work of staff. There should also be an awareness of the fact that what they do, and how they do it, affects the volunteer.

- Staff is generally responsible for the atmosphere of any agency ... , is it one in which an individual — whose primary motivation is "psychic income" (good feelings) — could thrive?

- Staff should be involved in the team building efforts, and made to realize that **volunteers do not threaten their jobs.** If a staff job is eliminated it says more about the economy than anything else. If they are eased out it is probably because of their inability to handle the job or get along with the co-workers .. not because a volunteer is in the wings.

- Volunteers do not take jobs away from a community. They are doing tasks which either would not get done (Little League, Girl Scouts, 4-H, Junior Achievement, Meals on Wheels, etc.) or would have to be handled by an individual already overburdened. In fact, they often create jobs through innovative projects.

- The fact that volunteers are putting in hours in no way affects the rate of unemloyment. As a matter of fact a great percentage of volunteers, particularly Board members, are people who work full time and give volunteer time in addition.

- Staff needs to be in on planning, and a part of decisions which affect them. They, too, need to feel they are a part of things, needed and appreciated. They must realize *they serve as the "constant"* in an otherwise changing situation. Day after day volunteers come and go, do what they can and leave ... but staff remains, and the continuity they provide is invaluable.

- Everyone involved should have an annual review of the goals and objectives of the organization and to see how these affect the staff and volunteers; what specifically is expected of each should be clarified with all concerned.

- Many a dedicated, dependable volunteer has moved on to another agency for lack of understanding, sympathy, or appreciation by staff ... but you can't share from an empty cup — these staff people must first feel good about themselves and what they are doing.

- Training is needed on all levels. Even those of us who train, if we're good, and care, continue to participate in training sessions developed by others and to increase our knowledge and expertise.

Job descriptions and an agreed-upon contract can help facilitate the activities of an organization, to assure satisfaction for the volunteer, and to clarify the expectations held by all.

GUIDELINES FOR VOLUNTEERS

Volunteers are people who give of their time in service to their community. In addition, they have a unique opportunity to serve as interpreters between the community and its agencies.

Volunteers should:

- Carefully choose the area in which they wish to work. Jobs suited to their interest and abilities are likely to be most rewarding.

- Realistically estimate the amount of time they have to give. Time commitments should be honored.

- Expect to arrive at their assignments at the agreed time. If they must be absent, they should call as early as possible to be excused, and if feasible, provide their own substitutes.

- Be clear as to what their roles and duties are, and they may request written job descriptions. Volunteers should expect continued guidance and direction.

- Expect to participate in orientation sessions, and should be urged to attend training programs. If volunteers find their time is not well spent, they should discuss the situation with the person in charge.

- Respect the principle of confidentiality and follow the same ethical standards expected of all staff members.

- Approach their working situation with open minds. If there is any procedure they do not understand or agree with, they should ask questions.

DEDUCTIONS

IRS — "The cost of transportation from a volunteer's home to where he serves is deductible." — Keep track of your mileage and figure credit according to current IRS guidelines.

- "Reasonable cost for meals and lodging"
- "The cost of attending a religious conference as a delegate"
- "Cost of upkeep of uniforms"
- "Unreimbursed expenses directly connected with and solely attributable to voluntary service performed for one's church or synagogue"
- "Use of personal auto — gas and oil or standard mileage for parking and toll fees"
- "Travel expenses in excess of allowance provided"

Actual deductions will differ with each agency and considerable national lobbying is being done to try to affect overall rules and regulations in this area. Contact your nearest IRS office for current rulings.

CONSIDERATIONS FOR A VOLUNTEER CONTRACT

Possible objectives for a Volunteer Contract:

1. To spell out, clearly, the expectations of the agency for the participation by the volunteer (including such things as uniform policies and number of hours).

2. To delineate the responsibilities of the volunteer as seen by the agency, for specific assignments.

3. To establish limits of authority, as well as the lines of authority for the volunteer, and the liability they could face.

4. To indicate the area of support which will be provided by the agency to the volunteer, such as orientation and training.

5. To clarify the extent to which volunteer expenses are covered by the agency, as well as how to record expenses for personal tax credit.

Additionally:

- It should be designed to meet the specific needs of the agency, and may vary for different types of volunteers within the organization.

- This tool should be filled out TOGETHER, so that any area of confusion is clarified immediately.

- It should be a tool of *assistance* and assurance that the needs of both the volunteer and the agency will be met. It should not been seen as something which will be held over a willing volunteer.

- It can be an effective device for both Leadership and Career Development.

- For the "gratuitous employee" (one working under direction and with supervision of action controlled by an agency or organization — without remuneration) defined working limits may be needed to establish legal responsibility in case of an accident.

GUIDELINES FOR VOLUNTEER CONTRACT

Agency Name   Form #
                                                              Date

AGENCY VOLUNTEERS

Name: _____ Social Security # _____
     Last   First   Middle

Address: _____/_____ Date of Birth: _____ Sex: __

Phone: Home _____Work _____

Organization represented (if applicable): _____

Current occupation: _____

Previous volunteer experience: _____

Applicable professional experience: _____

Applicable educational background: _____

Particular interests or hobbies: _____

Why would you like to volunteer here? _____

What type of service would you prefer? _____

Please indicate the days of the week and hours you could serve:

Day: _____ From: _____ To: _____ Time Limit

Day: _____ From: _____ To: _____ of Commitment: _____

Do you have a current license? # _____ Chauffeur's? _____

Do you have transportation? ____ Could you furnish it for others? ____

Do you have minimum automobile insurance required by law? _____

In case of emergency, please notify: _____

   Address _____ Phone: _____

Job description: _____

Supervisor: _____ Phone: _____

Areas of responsibility: _____

Limit of authority: _____

Specific expectations: _____

Assigned schedule: Day: _____ From: _____ To: _____

               Day: _____ From: _____ To: _____

Where you can go for help: _____

Orientation program: _____

Training available: _____

(If confidentiality is involved, a paragraph of policy would be appropriate, as would guidelines about dealing with the press).

Signed: _____   _____
      Volunteer   Supervisor

Date: _____   Date: _____

2. Meetings

"Haven't we met before?"

M eetings are often held by committee, and very often this is where the
real business takes place. Board and organizational decisions are
based on the transactions in committee meetings. F. Allen has been quoted
to say a committee is "A group of the unprepared, appointed by the un-
willing, to do the unnecessary." If this is true, no wonder people complain
about meetings!

GUIDELINES FOR CALLING A MEETING

Before having a committee meeting be sure that it is a committee that is
truly needed. If it is, there can be realistic objectives set and the chairman
will have a job description that makes sense. He should also follow some basic guidelines when calling any meeting. These include:

- Stating the reason for the meeting (on an agenda form, post card, or at
  least in a call to the participants)

- Setting the standard (by arriving on time and coming prepared)

- Developing an awareness of group dynamics (and seeking to make everyone comfortable and feel a part)

- Arranging for a written report of the transactions for the record (whether formal minutes, an interaction Memo or simply a set of notes in a
  notebook).

Far too often meetings and subcommittee meetings are held; grand and wonderful plans made, and actions taken — with little or no communication with others in the organization who may be affected by the decisions. Always keep the Executive body apprised of your activities so it can coordinate efforts among committees. Notify the membership at large, preferably through a newssheet, but at least at the general membership meeting.

MEETING CONSIDERATIONS

1. What are the needs, interests and expectations of the participants?
2. What is the agreed upon purpose of the meeting? (to train, inform, plan, decide, etc.)
3. What materials are needed to facilitate the meeting? (and who will handle them? agenda, handouts, visual aids, etc.)
4. Are additional resource people needed? (who? who will contact them?)
5. What activities can best be used to achieve the stated goal? (brainstorming, survey, discussion, buzz sessions, etc.)
6. Is there enough time beforehand for everyone to prepare adequately?
7. How much time will be needed to deal with the issues? (agenda should be planned with consideration for this).
8. What commitments do you seek and from whom?
9. Where could the meeting most effectively take place? (home, office, conference room, on site)
10. Who will be responsible for room arrangements, refreshments, clean up? (secure commitment)

RESPONSIBILITIES OF THE CHAIRMAN

- *Plan meetings in relation to objectives*
  Good leadership begins before the meeting, with plans for time, method and resources for accomplishing the stated goals.
- *Plan meetings in relation to what members expect*
  A well planned agenda is essential, but success depends on the participants having the information in advance, with time to prepare.

- *Define and clarify goals during the meeting*

  Without a clear understanding of the direction the group is taking, problems are likely to develop and members may become bogged down in unrelated discussion. Open with a review of the meeting's purpose.

- *Appraise progress mid-stream;* it's never too late to choose a new direction

  It is important that everyone understand what's been done and what remains ahead, who is responsible and what the deadlines are (see Objective Setting). Periodic progress reports are useful.

- *Use suitable methods of procedure* (see Problem Solving)

  It is important to address the problem from the most realistic approach. Different circumstances lend themselves to different approaches.

- *Evaluate*

  Don't let this worry you. It doesn't mean to be critical of the people or of yourself. It means to consider the *process* critically to determine its effectiveness or lack of it.

- *Communicate*

  Make it a habit to use active listening techniques (see Listening) to assure that what you are saying is what you mean, and what is being *heard* is what is intended.

- *Determine "decision-readiness"*

  Use caution before calling for a vote. The group may have too little information or feel unsure of its implication. Premature action may also come about if the leader fails to bring out inner, unexpressed concerns of reticent members. Dissatisfaction may follow.

- *Create new jobs as needs arise*

  An effective leader realizes when it is time to create a new job, (with appropriate recognition).

- *Divide jobs and responsibilities*

  A reasonable division of labor will ease the pressure on currently involved members and will offer opportunities to others for involvement and growth. Overburdening current staff will only burn them out prematurely.

- *Discuss problems openly* (see Conflict Management). Conflicts or anxieties should be acknowledged openly and discussed frankly.

- *Face tension frankly* (see Conflict Management)

  Often the surface reason for tension may actually camouflage the real reasons; every attempt should be made to air these concerns.

- *Set a climate of free expression*
  When members feel inhibited, or lack confidence or trust in the group or the leader, the session has less chance of being successful. People are more apt to express themselves honestly in an atmosphere of informality, friendliness and mutual respect (see Leadership).

GUIDELINES FOR COMMITTEE CHAIRMEN

1. *Provide an orientation session for your members*
   A. Allow time for getting to know one another (see Team Building Exercises and Icebreakers)
   B. Discuss your purpose and policies
   C. Explain committee structure and responsibilites
   D. Clarify goals and agree upon objectives (see Management by Objectives)

2. *Mail out a prepared agenda in advance of your meeting*
   A. Allow time for unfinished business
   B. List reports and who is responsible
   C. Schedule time with flexibility
   D. Carefully consider the order in which you place business on the agenda

3. *During meeting*
   A. Arrive early
   B. Begin on time (be sure a quorum is present)
   C. Keep the meeting moving and be sensitive to the needs of the group to be heard
   D. Keep the discussion on track and clarify frequently (or help the facilitator to do this)
   E. Motions should state:
      1. what is to be done
      2. at what cost
      3. by whom
      4. a prescribed time limit
      Be cautious not to tie yourself down with *unneeded* specifics

4. *When possible, set meeting dates well in advance* (so your project has priority on each member's calendar). An annual calendar, developed with all involved, can assure better attendance.

5. *Do not call unneeded meetings*

HOW TO ARRANGE AN AGENDA

The preparation of an agenda must be specific enough to make it truly useful to the participants. To simply list such things as New Business and Old Business really tells nothing. A well conceived agenda fully prepares the group for the business at hand and assures an expedient and productive meeting.

Sending out the agenda in advance allows participants to come prepared in spirit and materials. The members are mentally ready for the discussions and prepared with information or supplies appropriate to the issues. A chairman has a better chance of conducting a successful meeting if he sets the stage and reminds his Board or committee that he expects them to take time to review the agenda.

An itemized agenda helps the chairman or facilitator to stay on track and on time. The members should understand that you intend to stick by the time frames (unless the group as a whole chooses to alter the framework). Anticipating the possible reaction to each item by the group gives the chairman a chance to balance the issues on the agenda.

Matters of extreme importance or emotion generate the greatest, and often most time consuming, reactions. Each of these concerns should be considered when establishing an agenda so as not to run one heated item after another.

If the issues to be covered require a degree of knowledge this information should be provided in advance. An example of this could be an attached sheet listing Pros and Cons to a proposal. Additionally, if a committee has fully researched a question and is ready to bring a proposal for action to the Board for a vote, a brief background sheet should be included. This would highlight the points which were of significance in arriving at the proposal.

CONSIDERATIONS FOR AN ACTION AGENDA

1. State clearly what you expect to accomplish (the purpose of the meeting)

2. Specify a definitive amount of time for each item

3. Indicate *who* will be responsible as a resource for each item

4. Open with items of special interest and end with items worth staying for

5. Avoid:
  - Two time-consuming items in a row
  - Two items of high emotion coming back-to-back
  - Two similar subjects, one after the other
  - Two routine items in a row
  - Non-action items which can be covered in writing (attached to the Consent Agenda)

The idea is to balance the agenda to maintain interest and to encourage promptness and serious consideration of *all* significant items. Careful attention should be given to each item to determine whether it is appropriate to the meeting. (Some concerns are better dealt with on a lower level.)

A well designed agenda allows for *anyone* to facilitate the meeting. The responsibility lies with the Chairman to specify clearly what he hopes to cover, in what time frame, and to commit each active participant to provide needed background material and to serve as a resource for the period of discussion.

An Action Agenda is appropriately the second portion of any Consent Agenda. The Consent agenda facilitates the decision-making of routine or clear-cut issues. Treasurers' reports and minutes need not take up meeting time being read aloud. These are things which can be attached to the agenda and considered in advance of the meeting. Any corrections or additions can quickly be made prior to approval.

Items which require full involvement and final action should appear with specific time frames suggested. The ACTION part of any meeting is the real reason for convening the session ... not to simply *report out* what could be read at leisure and filed for future reference. The background, reference and quick attention items become part of the Consent Agenda.

THE CONSENT AGENDA

▲ Is a *time-saving* tool, which assures accuracy and opens up participation and communication. It is sent in advance of the meeting.

▲ It is *consent* because the participants of the meeting *consent* to accept:

The minutes (memo), which are *attached* and can be dealt with by correction or addition and a quick vote, but need not be read

The Treasurer's report, which can be attached and dealt with similarly

Proposals which require a quick vote- where the item is presented in exact wording and background information attached

The responsibility of coming prepared to deal with issues listed, having given advance thought to each item

The obligation to come prepared with items request (i.e. "please bring")

The responsibility to prepare fully to discuss issues they have said they would present at the meeting

The time frame presented *or* to mutually agree to alter it

▲ It is most useful when used with an Interaction Meeting which involves a Facilitator and Recorder and a common focus on a flip chart on which information is recorded with felt markers.

A meeting can have a ripple effect in that each person attending takes from that meeting positive, or negative, reactions. If the response is anger or frustration these feelings can then be taken out on family or co-workers. Their anger and frustration is one of the costs of an unsuccessful meeting!

By the same token, an effective meeting can have great benefits. Participants can return home or to their job rejuvenated, and happily motivated. Their good feelings can be shared much in the same way that "Courtesy is contagious". With improved meeting skills comes improved team work, communication, morale and productivity.

The Ripple Effect takes place simply because *any* process affects all who become involved, directly or indirectly. The aim of a good facilitator is to 'ease' the situation, to 'facilitate', to help good things happen.

An effective facilitator works at all times to remain neutral, to protect all participants, to help everyone to be heard accurately, to clarify and to seek consensus. The Ripple Effect in positive terms will register on the organizations effectiveness long after the close of a meeting.

CONSENT AGENDA FORM

Committee Name: _____

Date: _____

Place: _____   (directions if necessary)

Time: _____   (beginning and ending)

Facilitator: _____

Recorder: _____

Refreshments: _____

What to Bring:

What We Need to Accomplish:

Time assigned to each issue and person responsible for background material (yellow line the name when sending to an individual committed)

Action Items (Action Agenda)

i.e.: 9:00 Coffee and informal time
      9:15 Team building exercise — name
      9:30 First item — name
      10:00 Second item — name
      10:45 Third item — name
      11:15 Fourth item — name
      11:45 Establish next step (future plans)
           Assign individuals responsible
      12:00 Adjourn

Special Notes:

Resource Persons:

GROUP INTERACTION

If it distresses you that meetings never start on time, get sidetracked, and are inaccurately recorded, here are a few tricks of the trade.

The only way to start a meeting on time is to *start it when you said you would.* Gain a reputation for standing by the hour stated even if you must build in some social time: 9:15 coffee, 9:30 introductions. State it in your agenda and STICK TO IT!

This section is really about how to conduct a meeting so that the group is with you. It's a technique called "Interaction."

ALTERNATE WAY TO RUN A MEETING

Based on material by Doyle and Straus in "How To Make Meetings Work."

Interaction	Parliamentary Procedure
more informal, effective in smaller groups	formal, designed for large groups
leadership functions divided between chairman and facilitator	chairman is responsible for both content and process of meeting
stresses consensus and win/win decision making	uses majority vote, leading to win/lose decisions
recorder and group memory makes progress of the meeting visible and self-correcting	secretary takes notes privately for later use
group memo summarizes notes made and corrected at meeting	minutes written by a single member of the group, corrected at next meeting

INTERACTION MEETINGS

In an effective Interaction meeting each participant has a specific responsibility.

Role of Chairman: Active participant in group process
Make final decisions/set constraints for meeting
Establish the agenda
Speak openly for his own point of view

Deal with media and public in general
Responsible for assignment of tasks and deadlines
Represents the group in meetings with other groups

Role of Facilitator: A neutral servant of the group
Encourage participation from all attending
Coordinate logistics of meeting
Focus attention of the group on a common task
Refrain from evaluating ideas or participating in discussion
Protect all ideas from attack
Suggest alternate methods and procedures
Help the group find win/win solutions

Role of Recorder: Record and produce the Group Record (Minutes)
Refrain from participating in discussion
Write down basic ideas with felt markers on large sheets in front of the participants
Not to edit or paraphrase/use the speakers words
Make note of "Action" items with individuals responsible noted
Free ideas from the originator, unless his name is needed for a motion
Provide a common focus for the group
Post sheets, as completed, for later review (particularly by those coming late)

Role of Group Members: Keep the Recorder and Facilitator neutral
Make sure the information recorded is accurate
Establish "norms" for meeting
Determine the course of the meeting (May make procedural suggestions; may overrule suggestions of the Facilitator)
Give full attention to task of the meeting and to comments of fellow group members
Keep an open mind to new ideas and comments of others
Avoid becoming defensive

Group Record — This is the running record of the meeting, which allows the latecomer to see what has happened and what is going on now. As the minutes are recorded, no names are mentioned (except with assignment of tasks). These sheets are taped or pinned up where they can be seen by all. It permits the group to focus on the task at hand, rather than on each other.

"Action Items" are noted in another color next to the discussion item: i.e., "Check into possible meeting places big enough to accomodate 150 and available in mid-April. Carol T., by Oct. meeting."

Group Memo — This is what is usually the minutes — instead, it's a typed copy of the Record, dividing the information into What Happened and How, and Decisions/Action Items. (Yellow-line information specifically needed by an individual when mailing his copy to him). (See Group memo form, page 32).

The major advantage in conducting an Interaction Meeting is the opportunity for satisfaction by all attending. The objective is to establish consensus.

Consensus is a win/win solution that everyone can accept; a solution that does not compromise any strong convictions or needs. It is not a compromise, you do not give up something to gain something else. It may not be what you feel is the ideal, but on the other hand you don't really feel you are losing anything important.

Essential considerations in an Interaction Meeting are: *Content* — The WHAT (problem, topic, agenda) and, *Process* — The HOW (approach, method, procedure).

If consensus cannot be reached at least the group has made an effort and worked at collaboration. This experience is not lost. The members will have developed a real understanding of how much more productive the consensus approach is. It will become apparent that no one must lose in order for someone to win. Among the good things that come out of a consensus approach is the awareness each participant comes to that he is being *heard,* that his stand is being given a chance, that each option is being weighed objectively against an agreed upon criteria for success.

GROUP MEMO (MINUTES) SAMPLE

Commitee Name: _____

Date of Meeting: _____

Place: _____

Facilitator: _____

Team Building Exercise: _____

Members Attending:

What Happened and How:

Decision Action Items:

Future Plans (Next Step):

_____
(Recorder)

With questions call: _____ Phone: _____

MINUTES

I endorse Interaction Recording and the concepts outlined by Doyle and Straus (see Suggested Reading). Most committees could increase their efficiency as well as the understanding of the members if they saved Minutes for meetings larger than 30 and adopted the interaction approach to recording for smaller group meetings.

For those situations where minutes are essential, such as large general meetings, here are some key points to remember:

- At the beginning, identify the group or committee, the kind of meeting, date, time and place
- Identify chairman and secretary
- List those in attendance and state that a quorum was present
- Acknowledge the acceptance of previous minutes
- Give financial report as previous balance, total receipts, disbursements and present balance only (full report may be attached)
- Record all points of order and appeals for decision by the chair, whether lost or carried; secondary motions only when carried
- Note points of discussion when instructed to by the group
- Note that specific committee reports were given, cite key points only
- Separate subjects by paragraphs
- Identify any special speaker and the topic without further notation
- Cite actual count for or against in recording votes
- Identify each individual making a motion (those seconding need not be mentioned in the final draft)
- Close with the time of adjournment and sign the sheet. "Respectfully submitted" is outdated, as is the phrase, "turn over" the meeting or podium.

Minutes should be kept in a notebook, preceded by those of the previous years. A copy should always be sent to the Executive Committee.

To serve as an efficient and effective secretary, in the traditional manner, the individual should take careful notes. From these he will be expected to compile minutes. The material must be accurate, precise, impartial and specific. The final minutes should be typed and copies of them distributed within one week of the meeting. The president and committee chairmen should always receive a copy, and when deemed necessary, the committee as a whole should as well.

Minutes which are mailed in advance need not be read for approval at the following meeting, though corrections should be noted. When indicated in the record that an attachment will be included, it should be sent with the minutes.

Minutes should record what was done, *not what was said*. They should also include all motions, including amendments, in exact wording whether they passed or not, and who proposed them. These should be underlined. Motions which are adopted should be capitalized and appear with an asterisk in the left margin.

Minutes should *not* contain personal opinions or interpretations by the secretary, nor should they include descriptive phrases. Avoid adjectives and adverbs and concentrate on factual notes. Praise or criticism of members should appear only in the form of officially adopted notes of gratitude or commendation.

CHECK LIST FOR COMMITTEE CHAIRMEN

Careful consideration should be given by every new chairman to the many aspects of committee responsibility. The following is a useful tool for chairmen of small groups and organizations with little diversity. An adaptation of this form might be included in Board Orientation materials.

I. Committee Objectives

_____ Are the committee's (group's) objectives clearly stated and agreed upon by all?

_____ Are they realistic and pertinent to the purpose of the committee?

_____ Is it understood *who* is responsible for each objective and when it is to have been accomplished?

II. Committee Members

_____ Do they fully understand the function of the committee?

_____ Have you provided adequate orientation?

_____ Have you arranged for special training?

_____ Are they capable and motivated to carry out their assignments?

_____ Do you need a liaison member from a related committee to assure continuity?

_____ Are you on the lookout for potential leaders?

III. Committee Meetings

_____ Have the goals, date and time of each meeting been agreed upon (to meet the schedules of the members)?

_____ Have you set a routine for meetings and scheduled it well in advance?

_____ Have you selected a secretary, or do you plan to rotate the job of recorder?

_____ When additional people are needed, is it understood who will invite them?

_____ Do you report regularly from the Board to the committee and back to the Board?

IV. Committee Resources

_____ Are you cognizant of policies and bylaws applicable to your committee?

_____ Do you have all the needed tools to function effectively?
a. Past reports
b. List of the organization's goals and objectives
c. A list of committee goals and objectives
d. Minutes of previous meetings
e. A Board manual (where applicable)
f. A copy of current bylaws

V. Committee Reports

_____ Do you have concise reports for regular Board meetings?

_____ How do you keep the group as a whole informed?
a. Organization reports
b. Newsletter articles
c. Direct mailings
d. Area meetings

_____ Have you prepared an annual report that includes
a. Stated goals and objectives
b. Accomplishments

VI. Committee Evaluation

_____ Have you scheduled an evaluation meeting?

_____ How do you propose to evaluate?
a. Individual accomplishments
b. Fulfillment of committee objectives
c. Year's progress

_____ Have you established objectives and spelled out recommendations for next year's committee?

When an organizational meeting is held, and parliamentary procedure is essential, the following form can be very helpful.

PARLIAMENTARY PROCEDURE AT A GLANCE

TO DO THIS	YOU SAY THIS	May you interrupt Speaker?	Must You be Seconded?	Is the Motion Debatable?	What vote is Required?
Adjourn the meeting*	"I move that we adjourn"	No	Yes	No	Majority
Recess the meeting	"I move that we recess until..."	No	Yes	No	Majority
Complain about noise, Room temp., etc.*	"Point of privilege"	Yes	No	No	No vote
Suspend further consideration of something*	"I move we table it"	No	Yes	No	Majority
End Debate	"I move we vote on the previous question".	No	Yes	No	2/3 vote
Postpone consideration of something	"I move we postpone this matter until..."	No	Yes	Yes	Majority
Have something studied further	"I move we refer this matter to a comm..."	No	Yes	Yes	Majority
Amend a Motion	"I move that this motion be amended by"	No	Yes	Yes	Majority
Introduce business (a primary motion)	"I move that..."	No	Yes	Yes	Majority
Object to procedure or to a personal affront*	"Point of Order"	Yes	No	No	Chair decides
Request information*	"Point of Information"	Yes	No	No	No vote
Ask for a vote by actual count to verify a voice vote*	"I call for a division of the house"	No	No	No	No vote
Object to considering some undiplomatic matter*	"I object to consideration of this question".	Yes	No	No	2/3 vote
Take up a matter previously tabled*	"I move to take from the table"	No	Yes	No	Majority
Reconsider something Already disposed of*	"I move we reconsider our action relative to"	Yes	Yes	Yes	Majority
Consider something out of its scheduled order*	"I move we suspend the rules & consider..."	No	Yes	No	2/3 vote
Vote on a ruling by the chair*	"I appeal the chair's decision"	Yes	Yes	Yes	Majority

*Not Amendable

A CHAIRMAN'S GUIDE FOR CLIMATE SETTING

The following are key points for consideration before convening a meeting. In each case failure to demonstrate an awareness of the positive nature of each point will leave the leader open to possible negative results.

- People relate to each other more quickly in small groups.
- Exercises in sharing should be planned with the specific group in mind.
- Early questions should call for memories or experience readily available for everyone rather than opinions or ideas.
- It is effective if the leader will demonstrate first what he is asking others to do.
- It is important to allow for individual differences.
- The Chairman sets the stage; the attitude should be open and positive.

REASONS PEOPLE BELONG TO A GROUP

People do not associate with groups by chance, nor for purely altruistic reasons. People have needs, and membership in groups can satisfy any number of these.

1. A sense of being a part of something
2. A feeling of being wanted
3. An opportunity to work with others
4. A chance to give of one's self
5. A chance to use skills and talent

CHARACTERISTICS OF EFFECTIVE GROUPS

Each of the 13 points listed below represents a goal worth considering. None is easy, nor comes without conscious effort. However, each is important to the effectiveness of group efforts.

- The leadership is appropriate to the needs of the group, and members have confidence in their leader.
- Growth and welfare of all members are considered.
- Goals are clear and shared by all.

- Group goals are compatible with individual goals.
- A defined time-table is used.
- Communication is open, frank and non-threatening.
- There is a sense of agreed priorities.
- The resources of each member are used satisfactorily.
- Goals are high but achievable.
- Members are capable of handling the tasks.
- Decision-making procedures and authority are appropriate.
- Conflict is dealt with openly.
- Processes are routinely evaluated and results of those evaluations used.

HOW TO HANDLE TYPICAL PROBLEMS

1. Late-comers
- Make sure extra seating is closest to the door, near needed handouts
- Post "Group Memory" (see Interaction Recording)
- *Always* start on time — few people will show up late
- Don't make an issue of their tardiness but involve late comers at the first opportunity

2. Committee Reports
- Try using a Board Packet (print minutes and treasurer's report at beginning, following the agenda)
- Allow just 2 minutes for reporting committee chairmen
- Use visual aids or skits for variety
- Use a brief, standard "press release" form (see Publicity)

3. Lengthy Speakers
- State up front, the time assigned
- Notify speaker when there are 5 minutes left
- When requesting assistance, specify time allotted
- Sit near the speaker so you can tactfully cut him off

4. A Famous Guest in your midst
- Arrange some informal time in advance of the meeting
- Put him at the beginning of your program

- Provide a question-answer time
- Give him a chance to discover things about your group

5. How to Decide on a Resource Person

- Observe the person in another setting
- Review your needs with him in advance, by phone or in person
- Consider the evaluation of respected members who know him

6. How to Assure Everyone that Arrangements Will be as Requested

- Visit the site in advance, speak directly with those in charge
- Request a floor plan and map out your needs, on several copies
- Commit one member to arrangements
- Have a walk-through of your activities (at least mentally)
- Arrive early enough to deal with misunderstandings or changes
- Send a copy of your objectives and plan to all concerned

7. Apathy Among Members

- Divide into small groups to identify the nature of the problem
- Hold a structured discussion to isolate why members feel there is Apathy
- Allow a scheduled time to break into buzz groups to consider the issue
- Consider a group assessment survey which allows for anonymous responses
- Brainstorm for ideas to solve the identified problem

8. Participants Who Come Unprepared

- Be sure your agenda spells out preparation needed
- Set a good example
- Discuss openly the problem created and appeal for suggestions from the group
- On the agenda, run a yellow line over the individual's assignment to call further attention to it
- Always have specified deadlines
- Follow through. Let participants know what you expect of them
- Build on the positive; avoid dwelling on the negative
- Move on
- Learn to delegate to responsible associates (see Delegation)

EXERCISES — TO BUILD A SENSE OF TEAM

I. First Meeting — (Committee)

A. For 1 or 2 minutes, everyone is to guess the biography of one of the members. Family, skills, hobbies, employment, experiences, abilities, etc. At the end of the guessing, that person will tell how close the guess has come to the truth. The next person then becomes the focus. Repeat the process.

B. The leader offers Forced Preference Choices to the group. Each member is asked to select the one which most closely suits his outlook and move to one part of the room or the other. Each smaller group is then asked to discuss individual reasons for choosing that group. The process is repeated, with new choices, and regrouping for 5 or 6 options.

Suggestions:

I like to be seen as *efficient* or *friendly*

I would rather be a *chairman* or a *group member*

I prefer *making decisions on my own* or *with a group*

I tend to be happier working with a group or *working alone*

II. For Learning More About Old Colleagues (Committee)

A. 1. Have each group member fill out a 3 x 5 card in pencil with 2 "truths" and 1 "lie".

2. Shuffle the cards and one by one read the cards, allowing all members to guess, on a separate sheet, who each card represents. (Read all first, then go back — coding them — 1-2-3, etc.)

3. Acknowledge which card is yours and then let the members attempt to select the "lie" on their separate cards.

4. Share and clarify.

B. 1. Arrange members in subgroups of 4 or 5.

2. Ask each member to draw his lifeline with its up's and down's, highlights and disappointments, from the time he can remember to the present. Code each change of direction.

3. Ask members of each sub-group to explain their lifelines to one another.

4. Ask the members if they can discover any common threads in their experiences.

C. 1. Ask each member to write three things about themselves, each on separate cards

2. Place the cards in a basket and have each member select three (not their own)

3. Participants are then to find the individuals who filled out the cards they drew

4. When everyone has been identified the group sits down and each person takes turn giving his name. This is followed by the people with his cards each adding what they learned about him.

If you come out of your meetings wondering "What happened?", maybe it is time for you to become more involved, to take up the banner of Bear Bryant: *Cause something to happen!*" If you are in charge, decide what needs to happen and set about to accomplish this.

If you are simply a frustrated member, then speak to someone in charge. Describe your observations, express your concerns about the possible consequences, and if the listener is receptive, propose possible non-threatening positive solutions. But . . . cause *something* to happen!. Not to decide is to decide!. If *nothing* constructive is done, *something* negative will probably happen.

Everybody knows that there are three "bodies" in every group: *Somebody, Anybody,* and *Nobody.* When the Chairman asked for volunteers he said, "*Anybody* can do it." *Everybody* thought *Somebody* would, but *Nobody* did.

The *Somebody* decided that since *Anybody* could but *Nobody* did, then *Somebody* should and so he volunteered.

When *Everybody* saw *Somebody* doing what *Anybody* could, *Everybody* gladly lent a hand .. and soon the job was done!!!

YOU DO MAKX A DIFFXRXNCX

Xvxn though my typxwritxr is an old modxl, it rxally works quitx wxll; that is xxcxpt onx kxy. I havx oftxn wishxd that it workxd pxrfxctly. It is trux that thxrx arx 41 othxr kxys that do function wxll xnough . . . but just onx not working makxs a diffxrxncx.

Next time you think, "I'm only one person, my vote (or opinion) won't count" — remember, you do make a difference, and there is much in it for you if you'll speak up and contribute. You can't win the sweepstakes unless you enter.

RATE YOUR MEETING

Whether a leader or participant, you can determine how well your meeting works by evaluating the following "dimensions." After each item, circle the number that most accurately describes that dimension of your meeting:

1 — This is a problem area for us.

2 — We do "okay" with this, but could definitely improve.

3 — This is one of our strengths.

The higher your total, the more likely you already are having effective, productive meetings. The lower your score, the more likely you will want to read on and begin to apply some of the ideas presented here.

Making Decisions

Making decisions in a way that ensures both quality work and acceptance by participants is essential if a meeting is to be effective. Each of us wants to feel that we influence the decisions made in meetings we attend. The more closely a decision reflects a consensus of the group, the stronger the support and commitment on the part of individual participants.

1   2   3

Working Together

A group that works well together in meetings focuses on the task or agenda at hand and works to maintain adequate trust, involvement and support among its members. In order to function effectively a group must take care of its people as well as its agenda.

1   2   3

Organization and Procedures

Groups that meet successfully will have clearly understood organization and procedures so that participants know generally what to expect in terms of their group's operation. But it is essential that organization and procedures be flexible enough to deal with changing situations and information.

1   2   3

Goals

The goals for meetings are clearly understood and accepted by individual participants. What is to be accomplished in each meeting is clearly established, and the overall goals and purpose for the meetings are identified and articulated for the entire group.

1   2   3

Participant Resources

An effective group makes the best possible use of the ideas, suggestions, and strengths of individual participants. Their contributions will be invited and encouraged by the way the meeting is conducted. Members feel as if they are an essential part of the meeting process — which they are!

1   2   3

Communication

Groups that work well together maintain effective communication between both individuals and subgroups. Effective communication includes careful listening and thoughtful, clear self-expression. It means shared responsibility for being sure that information and meaning are exchanged fully and with understanding.

1   2   3

Leadership

Leadership in meetings that work is a shared responsibility. The person who is the designated leader recognizes and carries out his or her tasks, and individual participants look to themselves as contributing to the *leadership* of the meeting.

1   2   3

Conflict, Disagreement, Feelings

Effective groups regard conflict or disagreement and the expression of feeling as an opportunity to improve the meeting rather than something to be avoided. As a result, the meeting will be handled constructively in order to clarify positions or feelings so that these become new information available to the group as it works.

1   2   3

Process

In effective meetings, participants are aware of and pay attention to process, because it is an ongoing source of how well they are working together. This means paying attention to their immediate experience in meetings, and periodically evaluating the effectiveness of their meetings in "process" terms.

1   2   3

3. *Board Skills*

"How to Build a Better Board"

Volunteer organizations are formed in response to many social needs and may be sanctioned to offer social services, cultural or recreational programs, educational resources, or simply a "sense of belonging."

A Board of Directors has responsibility for the organization's operation, for stability, and for continuity. Community Boards can mean the difference between public understanding and support of volunteer efforts, and public apathy. Boards that understand their role and fulfill their responsibilities effectively can make a significant difference in a community.

Volunteers provide a quality of insight and caring which cannot be replaced by theoretical expertise or legislated services. The volunteer who feels needed and valued as a Board member will experience personal growth and continue to be concerned and involved in the community.

BOARD MEMBERS

Individuals who have indicated a willingness to serve as Board members should do so with full awareness of the obligations that accompany the position. In some situations the position implies simply dealing with policies and decisions which effect the organization. However, more often the position results from the fact that you are a committee chairman and are responsible for a particular project or activity for the group.

When the latter is the case, keep in mind that you'll be wearing *2 hats*. You will primarily focus your attention on executing the tasks related to your committee assignment, including the responsibility to report your progress to the Board. But you also need to give your attention to the activities of the Board as a whole, to weigh the issues presented by other chairmen. You can bring a needed perspective, a new *objective* one, to the proposals of others. Be prepared to exercise the obligation, to listen and to respond. The effectiveness of the Board's decisions depends on this.

Before expecting volunteers to join in your cause or support your organization, clarify your purpose. Why do you exist? What do you hope to accomplish?

CLARIFYING YOUR PURPOSE

Ten questions to ask when formulating a Mission Statement:*
1. Why do we exist?
2. What business are we in?
3. What is our most important product/service?
4. Who are our clients? ... volunteers? .. donors?
5. Why do they come to us?
6. How have we changed in the last five years?
7. What are our unique strengths?
8. What are our major weaknessess?
9. What philosophical issues are most important to us?
10. What would be lost if we ceased to exist?

*Based on material by the Public Management Institute

DUTIES OF A BOARD MEMBER

1. To exercise power for the benefit of the organization and all of its members with full honesty and reasonable efficiency
2. To exercise greatest care, skill and judgment
3. To act out of good faith and deal fairly with the organization
4. To display highest loyalty, reasonable care and business prudence in regard to the interests of the organization

What does this mean?
Diligence:

- Members of the Board should be fully aware of the duties and obligations of their positions.

- Board members should be able to devote the time necessary to fulfill their responsibilities.

- Board members should actively take part in the Board's decision-making process.

- Members of the Board should actively oversee the action of their organization.

- Members of the Board must scrutinize the official records and financial statements of their organization and question subordinates about them in a way that would be deemed reasonable.

Prudence:

This involves the avoidance of acts demonstrating lack of loyalty or good faith. With regard to loyalty, a Board member's primary concern would be avoidance of conflicts of interest.

Board members can be held liable. The position should be taken seriously. Under the law yours is more than a name on a letterhead. (See appendix for additional information).

When developing a job description for the key members of your Board, the following guidelines should be considered and expanded. Beyond the general points made, a job description should specify those activities which relate particularly to the Board in question. This should be done because there will be differences. The requirements and expectations for a Board member for the XYZ Agency will very likely be different from those of the ABC Foundation. Conflict, confusion and duplication of effort can be forestalled by a clear job description.

RESPONSIBILITIES OF A BOARD MEMBER

Executive Director

1. Serve as chief of operations for the organization
2. Act as professional advisor to the Board
3. Recommend appropriate policies for consideration
4. Effectively implement all policies adopted by the Board
5. Fully and accurately inform the Board with regard to programs
6. Interpret the needs of programs and present recommendations on all problems and issues faced by the Board

7. Develop a budget with the finance committee and keep the Board posted on the budget situation

8. Recruit the best personnel, develop a competent staff, and supervise effectively

9. Develop and improve the staff

10. Assist the Board in developing and conducting community information and education

Board of Directors

1. Counsel and advise, sharing benefit of judgment, expertise, and familiarity

2. Consult with the Executive on all matters which the Board is considering

3. Delegate responsibility for all Executive functions

4. Hold the staff responsible to the Executive Director

5. Share all communications with the Executive Director

6. Provide support to the Executive Director and staff in carrying out professional duties

7. Support the Executive Director in all decisions and actions consistent with policies and standards of the organization

8. Hold the Executive Director accountable for supervision

9. Evaluate the work of the Executive Director, annually

10. Perform in a prudent and diligent manner

Board President

1. Provide leadership in expediting goals of the organization

2. Guide the Board in fulfilling its stated roles

3. Facilitate meetings to assure adequate discussion, in an organized manner

4. Invest the Board's time wisely

5. Represent the Board in supervising the executive director

6. Supervise the chairmen of standing committees

7. Represent the organization in matters which affect it

8. Develop the leadership potential of Board members

9. Enhance the organization's image in the community

10. Perform as an admirable role model for other volunteers

SELECTING NEW BOARD MEMBERS

- Questions a Board might ask itself before looking for new members:

  A. What do we need? (people with specific expertise, a fund raiser, money, influential names, minorities, workers, etc.)

  B. What do we expect? (spell it out — time, financial obligations, meeting attendance, committee work, etc.)

  C. Where are we going?

  D. Why are we doing this?

- Questions a prospective Board member might ask himself and the Board before making a commitment to serve:

  A. What is expected of me?

  B. What is the organization's purpose? The Board's purpose? Do I believe in it?

  C. What am I going to get out of this?

  D. Is this the challenge I'm looking for?

  E. Do I have the time?

  F. Do I have the expertise?

  G. Am I comfortable with this group?

An effective Board is one that enlists the collective wisdom of carefully selected members. Each member brings to this group unique knowledge, insight, skill and personal contacts. By working together a synergism takes effect. The separate ideas blend together to build a whole greater than the parts. In weighing alternatives, collective judgment brings a community perspective to issues at hand.

An effective Board interprets programs and builds support for the mission of the organization. Board members provide liaisons with the broad base of the community, while providing continuity for purpose and policy.

CONSIDERATIONS FOR A BALANCED BOARD

RELATIONSHIPS	Access to Community Leaders, groups																								
	Access to Neighborhood Leaders, groups																								
	Access to people with expertise																								
	Access to people with money																								
GEOGRAPHIC AREA REPRESENTED	County (name)																								
	County (name)																								
	City (name)																								
	City (name)																								
	At Large																								
	Immediate Neighborhood																								
AREA OF EXPERTISE	Public Relations																								
	Financial Management																								
	Fundraising																								
	Personnel Adm.																								
	Legal																								
	Evaluation																								
	Program																								
SANCTION	Medical																								
	Small Businesses																								
	Local Media																								
	Churches																								
	Corporate																								
	Political																								
	Education																								
	Law Enforcement																								
	Neighborhood																								
	Union																								
RACE OR ETHNIC REPRE-SENTATION	Caucasian																								
	American Indian																								
	Black																								
	Latin																								
	Asian																								
	Other																								
AGE	Over 65																								
	51-65																								
	36-50																								
	21-35																								
SEX	Female																								
	Male																								
	YEARS ON BOARD																								
BOARD COMPOSITION ANALYSIS	**BOARD MEMBER**																								

TERMS TO CONTINUE -- | TERMS EXPIRE --

When an individual agrees to sit on a Board he becomes a part of a group that may well provide great camaraderie, a chance to make a difference in the community for a cause he cares about, and a challenge to his skills. But Board participation also involves certain liabilities which each new member should consider carefully before accepting a position.

LIABILITIES OF A BOARD

Based on material from the Institute for Voluntary Organizations:
You have a responsibility to:

- Attend Board and committee meetings regularly
- Be familiar with the minutes of Board and committee to which you are assigned
- Be familiar with your organization's publications
- Treat the affairs of the organization as you would your own
- Be certain your organization's records are audited by a reputable CPA firm
- Be familiar with your organization's goals, objectives and programs
- Insist that all committee meetings are reported to the Board
- Know your organization's budget, budget process, and financial situation, as well as any committee to which you are asigned
- Know who is authorized to sign checks and in what amount
- Avoid self-serving policies
- Inquire, if there is something you do not understand or if something comes to your attention that causes you to question a policy or practice
- Insist that there is a well-established personnel program with a competent staff chief executive
- Avoid the substance or appearance of conflict of interest
- Be certain your organization is fulfilling all aspects of its not-for-profit and tax exempt status
- Insist on a written nominating procedure
- Monitor the community and professional image of your organization
- Be certain the policies are clearly identified and that the board acts on them as a whole rather than by action of a small group of individuals
- Know your organization: Board of Directors, financial condition, programs and staff before you accept membership

- Require that your organization have proper legal counsel
- Monitor the activities of your executive committee to insure it does not overstep its authority
- Insist on the Board having a policy relative to board volunteer liability
- (See appendix for additional material)

Be fully aware of the duties and obligations of membership before agreeing to sit on a Board. Request a clear job description. Take an active part in the decision making process ... even when the issue isn't one which personally affects you. Develop the "people skills" necessary to implement what you know to be good and just. *HOW* you do what you choose to do ultimately determines the success you experience in *WHAT* you do.

TYPICAL BOARD PROBLEMS

Most problems which develop within Boards stem from one of the five following areas. By identifying those which seem to face your group you are then in a position to begin to resolve the problem. Look at the list and consider what you might do to alleviate the situation, having isolated the problem. For example, if Board members seem unsure of the dimensions of their jobs perhaps it is time to begin to develop job descriptions for each position.

1. **Fear:**
    - Of looking inept to others
    - Of what others might think
    - Of not really being up to the job
    - Of lacking the needed information
    - Of expressing opinions (which might differ)
    - Of the others, because of who they are

2. **Lack of skills**
    - In working with others as a group & communication
    - In organization, administration and planning
    - In decision-making and problem-solving
    - In research and development
    - In being an effective participant in a meeting

3. **Lack of information:**
    - As to the dimensions of their job
    - As to the lines and extent of authority
    - As to their specific roles
    - As to their responsibility and accountability
    - Or fear of asking, or not knowing they don't know

4. Lack of training:

- Under the direction of an unskilled director

- No preparation for the specific responsibilities

- Presided over by an ill-equipped president

5. Lack of understanding as to purpose:

- Feeling Boards are rubber stamps and gathered for social reasons

- Failure to conduct annual Board Orientation

- Failure to identify needs and resources of members and how they fit with the direction of the agency

All too often money is not allocated for Board training, nor is time. Even experienced Board members need time to build a sense of team in a new group, with new people and new challenges. Board members need structured time in which to build a sense of trust, to develop pertinent skills, and to assess needs and opportunities. Board Orientation and Board Training should be at least annual events.

BOARD ORIENTATION

Why bother? A Board Orientation gets members functioning faster as a team; it clarifies levels of authority and expectations; it allows members to begin to feel a part of the group, and it provides individuals with tools for effectiveness.

A Board orientation should be held annually, when new officers are elected. This formality assures a sense of belonging and understanding. It gives each member an opportunity to develop a sense of team and to understand assignments, policies and expectations. It should begin with an Ice Breaker appropriate to the makeup of the group (see page 62).

When a Board meets it has a chance to feel and see itself truly as a group. This happens only when members gather in the same room to work on the same task. How the individual members feel about the group, how much they feel like a part of the team, and how committed they are will depend on what effort has been made to develop camaraderie among the members.

CONSIDERATIONS FOR BOARD ORIENTATION

The following is presented as a guide for developing a Board Orientation session, a checklist of things to consider including:

When:_____ Individual Responsible: _____

I. Assessment of Needs of Incoming Board Members (In terms of skills and specific knowledge)
   A. As individuals
   B. As a functioning chairman
   C. As an effective Board member
   D. As a good communicator
   E. As a member of the team

   (Knowledge the executive committee should have in advance of orientation)

   What strengths do they bring to their positions?

II. Information on How Boards Work
   A. Existing jobs and responsibilities of each member
   B. Relationships which exist (Publicity guidelines, inter-organization communication, liaisons, etc)
   C. How individuals and committees communicate within the structure
   D. How decisions are made, policies set, planning accomplished
   E. Current Board and committee objectives and their inter-relationship

   (Material that should be provided in a Board Orientation packet)

III. Board Responsibilities/Committee Responsibilities (and a roster of Board members)

   (Outlines that should be included in the Board Orientation packet)

IV. Building a Sense of Team
         of confidence
         of self worth

   (Involve members in an activity and review the reasons for their on-going, conscious concern for their committee members)

   V. Information on
      A. Group process
      B. Situational leadership
      C. Roles of a Board member
      D. Communication/Motivation
      E. Decision making
      F. Problem Solving
      G. Conflict management

(Either as resource material or by way of active involvment in concepts with a visual presentation of ideas)

   VI. How To Make Meetings Work
      A. Interaction Meeting explanation
      B. Consent agendas and how to structure an agenda
      C. Group memo and minutes
      D. Your first meeting as a Chairman (purpose, duties, interrelationships, responsibilities, history, on-going activities, policies and procedures, objectives and a review of expectations-yours and theirs

(An explanation and review of these concepts)

   VII. Parliamentary Procedure at a Glance   (Resource material)
   VIII. Information at a Glance/ Review of Board Manual   (Resource materials)
   IX. Office procedures   (Resource material)
   X. Financial Procedures   (Resource material)

A review of your mission statement could be considered as one of the first activities in any orientation. All too often there exists a discrepency between members as to the exact purpose of both the organization AND the Board. For this reason it is important to establish agreement among the Board members early in their association.

A second step in this process is to break down the focus areas, which may be identified as committees. Perhaps some committees were formed decades ago and no longer serve a useful purpose. On the other hand, you may discover the need for a committee that has never been set up, but which would help facilitate the current mission, and established goals.

At this point Board members could generate ideas as to:

- The purpose and goal of the committee (Description)
- Realistic objectives (which are measurable)
- Factors working in your favor for successful achievement of these objectives, and
- Obstacles which you should anticipate and may have to be overcome

- The money, manpower and time needed to achieve the identified objectives

- The skills needed to succeed on this committee

- The skills to be acquired through participation on this committee

- The training which might be needed

- And, the line of authority for decisions

For any Board member to succeed as a chairman he needs a well defined job description. Much time is lost, confusion created and unnecessary conflict developed simply because there was no clear understanding on the part of Board members and their president as to what was expected of the other.

Ideas for integration on to a new Board include:

- Assign a sponsor to look after new members, make introductions, answer questions

- Arrange for informal social time, either in conjunction with Board meetings or by special arrangement

- Lead a tour of the agency or organization's office, to acquaint the individual with the facility and the staff

- Prepare a packet explaining the mission/purpose, policies, programs, committees, bylaws, budget, personnel and expectations, along with an organizational chart

- Give the new member a specific job to do! When he has a chance to make a contribution he becomes personally involved

- Offer skill training to alleviate any apprehension about doing the job

JOB CLARIFICATION

Position: _____

Tasks Performed on the Job	To Do This Task, a Person Must—		
	Know About	Be Able To	Believe or Feel That
Time commitment:	Monetary commitment:		

BOARD AND STAFF ORIENTATION

I. Responsibilities:
   A. Relationship should be understood (a balance should be created for viability and consistency); include an organizational chart
   B. Expectations of each should be identified and fully clarified (who determines policy, administers operations, plans program delivery, delivers program, recruits new Board members, establishes salary, evaluates organization results, assesses problems, approves budget)
   C. Areas of responsibility should be included in a Board manual
   D. Job descriptions should be developed, including skills needed and skills gained
II. Team Work
   A. Principles of partnership
      1. Honest, open communication
      2. Atmosphere of mutual confidence
      3. Identification and agreement on the mission of the organization
      4. Clarification of responsibilities (above I)
   B. Communications
      1. Reason for working together understood:
         To augment, not aggravate
      2. Clarification of interdependence
      3. Commit members to a group process, and develop an interaction approach
      4. Acknowledge that they are accountable as a unit
      5. Develop an understanding of roles and develop authority

BOARD MANUAL

This notebook provides the Board member with an easy resource for understanding and clarification. It should be distributed at Board Orientation.

Checklist for Board Orientation Manual
   1. Organization's purpose statement
   2. Constitution and By-laws
   3. Organization's goals and current plans
   4. Annual report
   5. Budget and financial report

6. Program description/goals and objectives

7. Organizational chart (staff names and numbers)

8. Committees (standing or ad hoc) and their goals and plans

9. Any evaluations conducted during past year

10. Personnel roster

11. Personnel policies and expectations

12. Board list — with identifications and phone numbers

13. Meeting information: days, dates, length of meetings, place

14. Minutes from meetings for last fiscal year

15. Any appropriate procedures governing conduct of meetings

THE BOARD PACKET

A Board packet is pertinent material that is distributed in advance of the meeting. It allows members to come prepared and to communicate their intent more accurately.

1. What It Is:

- A communique that brings you (the Board) up to date on committees' actions since the last meeting.

- It includes each committee chairman's report, minutes and financial reports as well as items that will come to a vote.

- And action items appear with the proposed motion, background and pro's and con's.

2. What It Does:

- Saves time — Minutes, Corresponding Secretary and Treasurer's reports, special dates, announcements and information are printed and reviewed for questions or discussion instead of being read aloud. Brings Board up to date and eliminates need for committee chairman to report, unless he has an Action Item.

- Improves decision making — The packet provides important background information on committee recommendations that will be discussed at the Board meeting. Board members who have read the packet materials are prepared for focused and intelligent discussion and action.

3. How it Works

- Board members request ahead of time that information pertinent to their reports, be included in the agenda. Example: If a motion is to be presented, the motion should be stated with any background information necessary.
- The agenda for the meeting is included in the packet. The agenda can be divided into two parts:
  * Consent Agenda items are included here. They require no discussion or decision. Items such as correspondence listing, announcements from committee Chair and the Treasurer's report could be included. A Board member may request that an item on the Consent Agenda be removed and placed on the Action Agenda.
  * Action Agenda items included here are motions to be voted on, reports from Project Chairs, Ways and Means reports. Additional old business and new business.
- An individual needs to be ASSIGNED to collect and assemble the information monthly as well as to distribute it to each Board member. This can be mailed or it can be the responsibility of each Board member to pick up his or hers at a designated time and place.

4. What You Do:

- Anticipate Board meetings — Plan your committee meetings so that recommendations or anything requiring Board action make the workbook deadline.
- Come to the Board with solutions or proposals — not problems. Include brief background and summary of pro's and con's. Write out motions.
- Type your material. Put name of committee and chairman, your phone number and date at top of page. Outline form is fine. Be brief.
- Deliver material to Secretary, or person assigned, 10 days prior to Board meeting.
- Obtain compiled packet material from Secretary, or assigned person, a few days before Board meeting.

Meetings are thus expedited, and many items put in writing which serve not only as a reminder to members, but assure accuracy of information. This packet should be kept in an on-going Board notebook.

TEAM BUILDING

Individual needs, group needs and task needs are all present during any group interaction. Because personal needs are strongest in the beginning, and because until they are met, the group never really moves on. It is important to take time in the beginning to build a team.

Members should be helped to become oriented to the personalities within the group and the expectations of the group. After this takes place, each is better able to answer whether his personal needs will be met in this group.

And here lies one of the key problems. If you have a chance to become *oriented* early in the life of the group you will have a far better chance of later achieving gratification from the group. If, on the other hand, you come time and time again and never seem to know where the group is coming from, where it is going, or how you fit into the scheme, then you are more apt to experience a degree of frustration. This frustration will prevent you from concentrating on the group needs, and you will be unable to make a meaningful contribution.

The *task needs* are the surface needs which bring us together in the first place — but it is difficult to focus on these objectives if there is conflict on the more basic level, involving *the process.*

Team Builders are essential to assure that groups work together with a common focus. Even if the members know one another, there is no guarantee that for any one project they will truly feel like a team. Investing time at the beginning of each meeting for a team building exercise will reap substantial rewards in the long run. These need not be "cutesy" or too involved.

Team building exercises are most practical for committees or groups of fewer than 30, and they differ from "icebreakers" in that icebreakers are designed to introduce the members and set them at ease. Team Builders help participants get to know one another better. If the people working together on a task do not feel like a team, they won't perform like a team.

On the other hand, once you develop a team feeling within the group tension is reduced and support for one another is generated. Members begin to see how their responsibilities are integrated with, and dependent on, the success of the activities of the rest of the group. Frustration with co-workers diminishes as members become more open to sharing success and concerns with one another. They also develop an understanding of the obstacles the others are facing.

The following represents a sampling of ideas for team building. I encourage you to adapt each to your group and to build into the exercises meaningful ideas or concepts. For example, if you are the core committee for the art auction, in the Forced Choice exercise you might ask them to divide by — a Picasso or a Rembrandt; a Calder or a Remington. If you're working on the Follies: a can-can girl or soloist; an emcee or a disco dancer.

Use your imagination and at all times be aware of the willingness of your group to devote time to such activities. If you introduce the idea on a positive note and periodicially demonstrate how it has helped, as a result of having taken the time to build a team feeling, those involved will begin to look forward to these activities. New ones can be tried by assigning this responsibility to different members each meeting.

IDEAS FOR TEAM BUILDING

1. Milling and matching
2. Art/Graphic exercises
3. Games/Contests
4. Round Robins
5. Sign Boards with information
6. Recall exercises
7. Treasure Hunt
8. Resource Hunt
9. Bingo for group characteristics
10. Sentence completion
11. Inventing with given objects
12. Mini-role play
13. Subdivision by common characteristics
14. Group or individual art projects
15. Private fantasy exercises
16. Partner interview
17. 1 minute biography
18. Group effort, collaboration
19. Graffiti board and discussion
20. Items for participant exploration

SAMPLE EXERCISES

1. Stand if you did any of the following over the summer (good for a first fall meeting of an existing committee or group). Chairman reads:

- Left the country
- Suffered a sunburn
- Had house guests
- Learned something new (like water skiing)
- Got away alone with your spouse

2. Divide into buzz groups of 5 or 6, or go around the room allowing each member to participate, if the group is small, and have members complete a sentence — briefly:

- As a volunteer my greatest strength is . . .
- I'm uncomfortable when . . .
- I usually try to make people think I'm . . .
- I'm really concerned about . . .
- The kind of person hardest for me to get along with is . . .
- I love working with people who . . .
- In this group I have felt . . .
- If I had it to do all over again, I'd . . .
- I wish I could . . .
- It concerns me that . . .

3. Provide each participant with two 8½ x 11 sheets of heavy paper. On one each is asked to write something he feels comfortable doing and enjoys talking about; this he pins on his front. On the second sheet he is asked to put something he would like to know more about; this he pins on his back. The group then mingles during the coffee hour, using the sheets as vehicles for conversation.

4. Forced selection. With this exercise you line up the group in the middle of the room and ask them to go to the right for one choice and the left for the other:

Do you see yourself as:

a leader	or	a follower
a Cadillac	or	a Volkswagen
a rose	or	a wildflower
a glass of Tab	or	a glass of champagne
a designer outfit	or	a pair of jeans
a sunny day	or	a cozy evening

After each selection the subgroups should talk among themselves about why they made the choices they did.

5. Paired sharing. Take turns sharing with a partner:

- Two things you like about yourself

- One skill you feel you have
- One of your most satisfying achievements

6. To break down role barriers, have each participant take a turn walking across the room from point A to point B. The catch is that each must take a *different* path. Save those members with the most intimidating roles for last. Most of the formality will be dropped by the time the 30th person seeks to go still another way.

7. When you want to form several sub-groups, you could try giving each participant a paper with a song title on it. Everyone is asked to hum his or her melody and to locate the others in the room with the same tune. If you want 4 to a group, distribute 4 cards with the same song title or sound, 5 if you want 5, etc.

8. A good exercise when a little ego boosting is needed is one used effectively in groups that have worked together as a team for a while. The idea is to form a circle and focus on one person, while each of the others makes a positive statement about the individual. Repeat the exercise until all involved have been the recipient of praise. Or, if the group is too large, you can go around the room and tell something positive about the person on your right.

9. Another is to share with the group the last thing you did before coming to the meeting. It can be very revealing. Or, where would you like to be if you could be anywhere? Or, tell me something about yourself I couldn't know if you didn't tell me.

10. A more difficult but revealing exercise is to have members pair up and share an experience with one another that the individual felt especially good about — a feeling of accomplishment or achievement.

Team Building exercises and ice breakers can be used effectively on the committee level, and, with adaptation, with the group as a whole. Think creatively about what you might do to introduce ideas such as these into your organizational activities. The time invested in team building pays many rewards.

ICE BREAKERS

1. Paired Introductions
   Each person meets and gets to know one other person, and in turn introduces his partner to the entire group.

2. One Minute Autobiography
   Break into small groups (up to 10) and with a timekeeper, give each person 1 minute to tell about himself (not his job, family, town, hobbies — but attitudes and values).

3. Depth Unfolding Process

   In small groups give each member 5 minutes — the first 2 to share with the others what brought you to this point in your life, 1 minute to tell of your life, 1 minute to tell of your happiest moment, and 1 to answer questions (leader goes first).

4. Write a Press Release

   Write a press release about yourself and read it to the group. An alternative is to interview someone else and write a press release on that person.

5. Life Map

   Using a crayon, on newsprint, each person creates a picture of his or her life (with stick figures and symbols).

6. Name Circle

   Go around the circle saying your name and then repeating the names of all who have preceded you. An alternative is to state your name and explain how you got it.

7. Sandwich Boards

   On 1 large piece of newsprint each participant lists "Things I Know"; on a second sheet, he lists "Things I Want to Know." The two are joined with tape, sandwich board style, hanging one in front and the other in back. The participants then circulate informally getting to know one another.

8. Personalized Name Tags

   Let members create their own name tags. Provide: pens, 3 x 5 cards, old magazines, scissors and glue. Once created, they are asked to mingle and share with others why they chose the pictures they did.

9. Free Vacation

   Give everyone a 3 x 5 card and ask him to write where he'd rather be than here. Share.

10. Give everyone a length of yarn (these should be of varying lengths). Ask that they tell the group about themselves, talking for as long as it takes to wrap the string around a finger.

4. Group Process

"Two's Company. . ."

Group Process: The interaction the group experiences. It is important because it reflects the continuity, maturity, productivity and honesty of the group.

We assume different kinds of roles within different groups, depending upon how safe we feel and how interested we are in the task. These roles generally fall into two categories: task or maintenance. When we assume a *task role,* we are helping the group to accomplish its objective. We might do such things as coordinate, evaluate, give information, record information. *Maintenance roles* are the ones that help the group interact comfortably, so that the task can be accomplished in the most productive manner. When we assume a maintenance role, we do things like encourage, mediate, agree with, and congratulate individuals for good ideas. Some roles interfere with the task and maintenance of the group, such as: blocking others' comments, seeking recognition, dominating, and avoiding the point.

If we can learn to be aware of the group process and help others to be aware of it, we will accomplish more, and feel better about it. Several elements affect communication, and thus the effectiveness of the group process. These include:

1. Sense of significance (how much you feel a part)

2. Sense of control (how you fit, how you feel about your competence level)

3. Sense of openness (how well liked you feel)

It is important that we distinguish between *content* and *process. Content* is the "What". (agenda planning, the list of things the group needs to accomplish, etc.) *Process* is the "How". (brainstorming, lecture, slides, etc.) When we talk about group process, it is important to consider the process in terms of: *directionality, participation, leadership* and *climate.*

— *Directionality* - Who is talking to whom (i.e., one to one, leader to group, or aimlessly).

— *Participation* — Everyone should be actively involved.

— *Leadership* — It should facilitate interaction by encouraging and stimulating, rather than controlling the involvement.

— *Climate* — Should be one of cooperation rather than competition.

ROLES TAKEN DURING GROUP DISCUSSION

Whether intentional or not, individuals involved in groups take on roles which affect their behavior and thus the group process. Some are task roles, some maintenance, and others self-serving. Many of the latter can have a negative effect on a group. It is for this reason that I feel it important to learn to recognize and deal with the various roles which are manifest in a group.

A. Task Roles (Help get the job done)

1. Information or opinion seeker — Looks for facts and feelings on which to make a decision.

2. Information or opinion giver — Offers facts or generalizations which are authoritative, or relate to his own experience, pertinent to the group problem.

3. Clarifier — Rephrases for clarity and understanding.

4. Initiator — Proposes subjects, processes and direction.

5. Elaborator — Develops concepts more fully.

6. Orienter — Familiarizes group with new ideas, or new members with group.

7. Summarizer — Summarizes what has occurred, points out departures from agreed-upon goals, brings the group back to the central issues.

8. Evaluator — Subjects the accomplishments of the group to standards, or a set of standards, and questions the practicality, the logic and the facts.

B. Maintenance Roles (Help members feel satisfied and comfortable)
   1. Harmonizer — Mediates the differences among other members, attempts to reconcile disagreement, relieve tensions in conflict situations.
   2. Compromiser or mediator — Proposes possible solutions or approaches which will meet most needs.
   3. Encourager — One who encourages others to continue to be involved.
   4. Supporter — Has praise for everything and everyone.
   5. Gate keeper — Keeps communication channel open by encouraging or facilitating the participation of silent members or by proposing regulation of the flow of communications.
C. Self-serving roles
   1. Blocker — May be negative and stubborn, resisting, disagreeing, and opposing without reason.
   2. Dominator — Tries to assert himself by attempting to manipulate members of the group.
   3. Resister — Refuses to be put into a position of having to commit to anything.
   4. Aggressor or criticizer — Critical of everything and everyone to gain status.
   5. Follower — Going along with anything.
   6. Recognition seeker — Works in various ways to call attention to himself through boasting, unusual acts, or reporting of personal accomplishments.

NON-PRODUCTIVE BEHAVIOR

Some participants in groups regularly interfere with progress. The more common types of nonproductive behavior include:

- *Aggression:* working for status by criticizing or blaming others; showing hostility against the group or an individual; deflating the ego or status of others
- *Blocking:* interfering with the progress of the group by intentionally deviating from the subject of discussion; citing personal experiences unrelated to the problem; rejecting ideas without consideration; or arguing excessively
- *Self-confessing:* using the group as a sounding board; expressing inappropriate personal feelings or points of view that are not group oriented

- *Competing:* vying with others to produce the best ideas, to talk the most, to play the most roles, to gain the leader's favor
- *Recognition seeking:* attempting to call attention to one's self by loud or excessive talking, extreme ideas or unusual behavior
- *Special pleading:* introducing, or supporting suggestions related to personal concerns or philosophies; lobbying
- *Clowning:* joking; mimicking; disrupting the work of the group
- *Seeking sympathy:* trying to gain group members' sympathy to one's problems or misfortunes; deploring one's own ideas to gain support
- *Withdrawing:* acting indifferently or passively; resorting to excessive formality; daydreaming; doodling; whispering to others; wandering from the subject
- *Degrading:* acting in a manner which criticizes others

A clear understanding of behaviors that help or deter progress can help the leader and increase the effectiveness of groups, organizations and communities. Good facilitation, in an interactive setting, decreases disruptive activity and increases productive involvement. (See segment on Interaction Meetings.)

A considerable responsibility falls to the group leader to involve all participants in discussions which affect the group. The following is intended as a guide to stimulate productive discussion.

USING QUESTIONS TO STIMULATE DISCUSSION

Well phrased questions stimulate group participants to think and motivate them to discuss the issues at hand. Three basic factors affect stimulation and motivation:

1) Choice of the right question
2) Framework of the question
3) Directing the question

I. Choosing the right question:

A. The right type of question is dependent upon the results sought.
B. Categories of questions:
1) Factual questions:
- Used to get information
- Good for discussion starters
Example: "How many people are on your committee?"

2) Leading questions:
- Used to suggest an answer and have the group analyze
- Helps to broaden the discussion
  Example: "How would you feel about..."
3) Clarifying questions:
- Used to challenge old ideas and develop new ones
- To avoid snap judgments
- To help find real causes or answers
  Example: "What you are saying, then, is that committee apathy isn't a problem for you."
4) Hypothetical questions:
- Used to suggest or introduce leader's ideas into the discussion
- To test conclusions
  Example: "What would you think of having a follies?"
5) Alternate questions:
- To decide between two or more points
- To comparatively evaluate suggested solutions
  Example: "Are day or night meetings better?"
6) Overhead (General):
- Directed at the entire group
- Used to promote group thinking
  Example: "What might we do about this?"
7) Re-directed questions:
- Directed at leader but returned to the group
- Used to promote group activity
  Example: "That's a good question, Susan. How would you answer that in terms of your experience, Clare?"

II. Framing the question
A. Be brief
B. Cover a single point
C. Relate the question
D. Develop thinking from a constructive, positive point of view
E. Use words that are natural to you
F. Use words that have a clear meaning to the group

III. Directing the questions:
A. Direct questions to the group as a whole
B. If no response, then select individuals to respond

C. Allow sufficient time to reply
D. Do not hesitate to restate the question if the group expression shows confusion
E. Encourage members of the group to question one another
F. Direct a hypothetical answer back to the group if you get no response
G. Allow those who truly do not want to participate to listen

CHARACTERISTICS OF A GOOD QUESTION

A. Must have a specific purpose
B. Have relationship to what is already known
C. Be understood by the group
D. Emphasize one point
E. Require a definite answer
F. Discourage guessing
G. Encourage creative thinking
H. Use why, where, when, who and how...

IMPROVING QUALITY OF PARTICIPATION

Any group is strengthened and enabled to work more efficiently if its members:

- Become more conscious of the role function needed at any given time
- Become more sensitive to and aware of the degree to which they can help meet their needs through what they do
- Undertake self-training to improve their range of role functions and skills in performing them
- Become responsive to changing goals
- Become aware that what *appears* to be non-functional behavior may not be
- Become conscious of the positive possibilities of conflict aired within a group
- Become more concerned with the issues than the personalities

Some of the responsibility for effective group process must fall to the participants themselves. The material which follows enumerates ideas that can help individuals to become better group participants.

HOW TO BE A BETTER GROUP DISCUSSION PARTICIPANT
Based on material by Marty Squire, consultant
(used with permission)

1. Come prepared. If material has been sent out in advance of the meeting, that's when it is supposed to be read. Time is often wasted at meetings filling in members who *should* already be informed.

2. Arrive on time and stay until the end of the meetings. Consistently late arrivals and early departures carry the non-verbal message, "I have better or more important things to do." This is seldom well received.

3. Be attentive. If you thought the meeting was important enough to attend, then attend to it when you are there. Be aware not only of *what* is being done, but *how* it is being done.

4. Be perceptive. In particular, become more aware of the nonverbal messages that have an effect on the group — room arrangement, seating arrangement, gestures, eye contact, body movements. Call them to the group's attention when it would be helpful.

5. Help facilitate the discussion by taking an appropriate role in it. Typically, these are divided into roles which either contribute to accomplishing the group's task or making the atmosphere one which is conducive to openness, cohesiveness and satisfaction on the part of the members. By all means, avoid taking a self-serving role. (A list of roles is included elsewhere). If you see that a needed or helpful role is not being taken, take it yourself.

6. Be a contributor. Presumably, that is why you were asked to be a part of the group. If the group is a small one (up to 15 members), you have an even greater responsibility to contribute. See that your contribution is:

   a. Relevant to the discussion (if you have been actively listening, you lessen your chances of making irrelevant contributions!). Use the "hook-on" technique of prefacing your comment with a reference to something said earlier by someone else.

   b. Offered at an appropriate time. Don't wait until the middle of a vote to come up with another alternative!

   c. Long enough to make your point. (It has been found that contributions are more often too short rather than too long).

   d. Short enough to sustain the group's interest and attention. This means organizing your thoughts before you open your mouth. Don't belabor a point. Group members will remember this and then tune you out before you ever get started next time.

e. Clear and easily understood. This may require rewording, defining terms, giving examples. Get some feedback to let you know how you're doing.

f. Open to evaluation and criticism. Once your comments are offered, they belong to the group, not to you. Let the members know they are free to do what they wish with the contribution. Sometimes it helps if you are one of the first to criticize or evaluate it.

g. Informative and provocative. Don't bother if it isn't going to add something to the discussion or elicit further comments or ideas.

7. Don't be afraid to disagree. A certain amount of conflict is both inevitable and indispensable in a group discussion. The key is not to let it become personal. It is better to say "I believe that information may be incorrect" than "you are wrong", for example. If you are going to criticize the idea or the outcome ("Things didn't turn out as well as they might have", not "You sure let down your end"). If you are going to compliment, compliment the person, not the idea, the outcome, etc. ("You did a wonderful job on the Ball", not "The Ball sure was a success this year.")

8. Don't be afraid to be creative or innovative. Unfortunately, conformity is more often rewarded than creativity in an organization or group, but don't let this deter you! If you have gained the confidence and respect of the group, the members will usually be willing to at least hear a creative approach or innovative idea. Particularly if you back it up with sound reasons and answers to possible criticisms before the group starts to comment on it. Beat them to the punch!

9. Give anyone else's creative approaches a fair shake. You may see it as a wild idea but possibly that's the way someone saw your creative approach! Tolerance and open-mindedness are required along with a willingness to try something new.

10. Become more tentative and less positive and/or dogmatic. Keep in mind that:

a. Things are seldom either/or, always or never. There is usually some middle ground.

b. Times, conditions, situations change. Don't treat *any* of them as though they never do!

c. Your perception of reality, truth and goodness are always (there's one time that word is all right!) at least a little different from every one else's, but this doesn't mean one is wrong and the other right. You will find inter-personal relationships in a group or anywhere else are much smoother when you preface more of your comments with, "To me", "As I see it" or "As far as I know".

5. LEADERSHIP

"Take Me To Your Leader"

"Each time we ask more of ourselves than we think we can
give . . . and then give it . . . we grow."

Cicero

In effective relationships, whether boss with employee, staff with volunteer, or chairman with committee, there must be a *balance*. This should reflect how much both are getting out of the relationship. If one or the other tends to gain more, and this is conspicuous to the other, productivity diminishes. The power one has over the other is rarely dependent on purse strings alone. It is also dependent on *each* person in the relationship receiving his or her needed degree of satisfaction and gratification. That's what volunteer work is all about.

A leader has only so much power over others. It is useful, positive, creative power if it includes finding the best people for the jobs, people who receive in return for their giving. Meeting the needs of others, so they will meet yours, is one of the most important things a leader can do.

WHAT IS LEADERSHIP

What is leadership? It is situational. Different situations call for different styles of leadership. It is *the art of getting or inspiring people to do something* with the focus on people. By contrast, management deals with the allocation of resources associated with a *task*.

A leader is expected to act as a liaison between an individual and the organization. The behavior must be appropriate for the situation — and one style of leadership is not necessarily better than another. (Can you imagine General Patton as leader of a sensitivity group ... or Gandhi as a World War II commander?) Groups differ and so must their leadership.

Leaders integrate the needs of followers with the goals of the organization — integrating people with tasks. They TRANSPORT POTENTIAL INTO REALITY. When selecting individuals to take on positions of leadership remember *people skills* are more important than expertise in a specific area. Resource people should make up the committee — but not be expected to have leadership skills.

Leaders need to focus on the individual.

- Look at the needs and strengths of the individual, "Build from Strength" (Drucker).
- Everyone should have the maximum opportunity to develop and utilize his talents and strengths.
- Provide a "climate" in which members will be allowed to grow and accomplish (in the interest of the organization) the things of which they are capable.
- Provide every opportunity for members to identify their interests and abilities. When they know more about themselves, they are better able to share this with the leader. (A nominating questionnaire is one tool.)
- Accept a refusal. Forcing members into tasks for which they have no enthusiasm will lead to frustration and disappointment for all.
- Avoid overstaffing — to the extent that the individuals begin to feel they really aren't needed.
- Specify clearly your expectation of your members and listen to their expectations of you and your group.
- "Never entrust opportunity to a non-resource." Be aware of the *capability* and *dependability* of your members.

FIVE LEADERSHIP STYLES

When selecting a style, the maturity of the individuals and the group (in relation to the task) is the major concern. Considerations:

- Motivation/achievement/needs/expectations
- Willingness and ability to assume responsibility
- Education/experience/abilities

1. Authoritative ("Telling")
2. Political ("Selling")
3. Evaluative ("Testing")
4. Participative ("Consulting")
5. Laissez-faire ("Joining")

The first two are leader-centered, and the last two group-centered. The less maturity a group demonstrates, the more direction it will need.

1. *Authoritative* style demands that the leader decide and announce decisions
2. *Political* style finds the leader deciding and "selling" the decision to the group
3. *Evaluative* style allows the leader to present ideas and invite questions
4. *Participative* style requires the leader to present alternatives and the group to choose from among them
5. *Laissez-faire* style has the group defining the boundaries and making the decisions

To be successful as a leader, it is generally felt that the group as a whole should be involved in and "buy into" the decisions which will affect them. "Bottoms up" is a good rule. Consult the people at the bottom before inflicting decisions on them.

FUNCTIONS OF A LEADER

Each member is seen as having a responsibility to the rest of the group to help make the group effective. The leader coordinates the activities of the group. These include TASK FUNCTIONS (things which must be done if problems are to be solved) and MAINTENANCE FUNCTIONS (things which help the group stay together and feel good about working together).

Task Functions include:

1. *Initiating* — defining a problem, suggesting procedure for problem solving, making a proposal
2. *Seeking Information or Opinions* — requesting background data, generating suggestions and ideas, gathering facts
3. *Giving Information or Opinions* — offering facts or relevant information, stating beliefs, sharing new ideas or suggestions
4. *Clarifying or Elaborating* — interpreting others' ideas, clearing up confusion, pointing out alternatives
5. *Summarizing* — pulling related ideas together, establishing where the group is and what has been covered
6. *Testing Agreement* — checking to see if the group has come to a consensus, or has reached an understanding

These task functions will help in problem-solving and completing a task, but to be a productive, successful group, there are several maintenance functions which deserve consideration.

Maintenance Functions include:

1. *Encouraging* — being responsive to and accepting of others; listening and trying to understand
2. *Expressing Group Feelings* — being sensitive to how the group feels and being aware of inter-personal relationships within the group
3. *Harmonizing* — attempting to reconcile opposing points of view. Tension must be reduced before group members can explore their differences objectively
4. *Compromising* — admitting error if you make one, disciplining yourself to help maintain the group, offering to compromise your own position to help the group
5. *Gate Keeping* (active participation) — keeping the discussion a *group* discussion
6. *Setting Standards* — code of operation adopted by the group — such as policy of letting everyone have a turn to be heard

In assuming an active role, every member has the responsibility to help make the group effective — and to consider ideas, not their source. Here's where Interaction Recording works so well. The chairman, as well as each individual, has a responsibility to listen for understanding, to contribute and make suggestions, as well as to monitor himself so as not to dominate.

To put a group at ease, a leader can help members become better acquainted by using team building exercises. It is also important that members see one another easily. Sit *with* the group yourself, if you are leader.

The leader should show enthusiasm and concern for the tasks facing the group. Help the members to realize that it is a job in which everyone's participation is needed. Promote team work by setting an example of friendliness, understanding, fairness and good will.

An effective leader encourages the group to consider all ideas fairly, so no one is afraid to make a suggestion. Give recognition to all and work to include everyone in your discussion.

SOME NEEDS OF PEOPLE IN GROUPS

If you want loyalty, honesty, interest and the best efforts from your group members, take into account that . . .

- They need a SENSE OF BELONGING.
  a. A feeling that no one objects to their presence
  b. A feeling that they are sincerely welcome
  c. A feeling that they are honestly needed for themselves, not just for their hands, their money, or to make the group larger
- They need to have a SHARE IN PLANNING THE GROUP GOALS. Their needs will be satisfied only when they feel that their ideas have had a fair hearing.
- They need to feel that the GOALS ARE WITHIN REACH and that they make sense.
- They need to feel that what they are doing contributes something important to HUMAN WELFARE — that its value extends beyond the group itself.
- They need to share in MAKING THE RULES OF THE GROUP — the rules by which together they shall live and work toward their goals.
- They need to know in clear detail just WHAT IS EXPECTED of them so that they can work confidently.
- They need to have RESPONSIBILITIES THAT CHALLENGE, that are within range of their abilities, and that contribute toward reaching their own goals.
- They need to SEE THAT PROGRESS IS BEING MADE toward the goal *they* have set, and that they are making progress toward their other personal goals.
- They need to be KEPT INFORMED. What they are not up on, they may be down on.
- They need to have CONFIDENCE IN THEIR LEADERS AND OFFICERS — confidence based upon *assurance of consistent fair treatment*, of *recognition when it is due*, and of *appreciation for steady, contributing membership.*

In brief, regardless of how much sense the situation makes to the leader, it must also make sense to the members.

Many feel the need for these REWARDS:

- To enjoy feeling useful — their only "pay" is satisfaction in a job well done
- To use their special skills and talents
- To appreciate the incentive for education
- To have the opportunity to grasp local and national issues
- To experience personal growth and intellectual activity

DELEGATING

It has been said that delegating is the hallmark of a successful leader. It is a method of getting work done with each member doing his part. Through delegating we assign a part of the responsibility to others ... and ask them to find solutions. By doing this, we also save time (see Time Management).

1. **Considerations before Delegating**
   - Is the individual capable of handling the task?
   - Will the individual take the responsibility seriously and feel a commitment to it?
   - How critical is it to the total operation that this task be done well?

2. **Criteria for Delegation**
   - The ability of the individual to handle the task
   - The importance of the task
   - The consequence of failure
   - The relationship of those involved

3. **Advantages of Delegating**
   - Develops a sense of belonging and importance in the members involved
   - Encourages creativity, initiative and independence
   - Inspires motivation (stimulates)
   - Shares the power
   - Offers an opportunity for growth and development, and for others to observe this change
   - Allows the leader freedom to oversee the total operation

4. **Responsibilities of a leader**
   - To assign tasks only to those qualified
   - To make the assignment clear
   - To assign authority to discharge the tasks
   - To obtain the member's commitment to the task
   - To provide needed resources in order to accomplish the task
   - To offer encouragement and support

LEADERSHIP AIDS

A clear understanding of how an auxiliary or group is organized, how it operates, and how it serves the community, is essential for all members, but it is especially important for those leaders in national, state and county positions.

The following questions may be helpful in making and implementing plans.

1. What goals have you set for your auxiliary or group? Do you have a "mission statement"?

2. Are your current activities consistent with the purpose or goal?

3. What is the degree of membership involvement in your current programs and projects?

4. Are your activities in keeping with community needs? If not, what programs and projects might be substituted for your current activities?

5. Does your present auxiliary or group structure lend itself to effective programs and projects? If not, what changes should be made?

While you are fulfilling the duties as president or chairman, consider the future of your organization by building leadership qualities in others. Ongoing skill training is one of the best ways to develop the leadership potential of your members.

HOW TO KEEP DISCUSSION ON THE TOPIC

A leader must see to it that the key ideas are discussed and seek the maximum value out of each point made. The skill that helps most is *appropriate questioning.* Members of any group bring a variety of skills, information, and degrees of motivation to the group, and, as a result, they do not always operate at peak efficiency without help from the leader.

When to ask questions is particularly important. Here are five specific reasons:

1. *To focus the discussion:* Individual statements usually have a point, the statements themselves relate to a larger point being made, and the general discussion relates to an issue or to an agenda item. Use questions to determine a speaker's point or to determine the relationship of the point to the issue or agenda item.

2. *To probe for information:* Many statements need to be developed, supported, or in some way clarified. When the point appears important, the leader should pose questions to help bring the ideas into focus.

3. *To initiate discussions:* During a discussion, there are times when lines of development are apparently ignored, when the group seems ready to agree before sufficient testing has taken place. At these times, it is up to the leader to open up additional discussion and consideration by asking key questions.

4. *To deal with interpersonal problems:* Sometimes there is a need to ventilate very personal feelings. When this happens, the leader should help the individual air his feelings, but not let his bias interrupt the real purpose of the discussion. At times, the group begins to attack a *person* instead of the *information* that is being presented. When this happens, the leader has the burden of focusing attention of the group on the idea, instead of the source.

5. *To choose/commit/decide:* To select from a number of options, to commit participants to responsibility, or to decide on a direction.

Questions by themselves will not make a discussion. In fact, some questions can hurt the discussion that is taking place. An effective leader uses questions sparingly, but decisively, and develops sensitivity to the needs of the group members. He can 'read' tone and inflection and body language, as well as words.

RESPONSIBILITIES OF A LEADER

- Listen!
- Contribute
- Do not dominate
- Show enthusiasm
- Put group at ease
- Promote team work
- Discourage criticism
- Focus on problem or task, not personalities
- Be fair
- Give recognition

CONSIDERATIONS FOR LEADERS

Based in part on material by Philip B. Crosby in The Art of Getting Your Own Sweet Way, @ copyright Philip B. Crosby (used with permission)

Philip Crosby offers a number of concise points worth noting, with regard to Leadership. These include:

- There are no easy solutions.
- Prevention is a future thing.

- People are more important to situations than things.
- Embarrassed kittens become tigers.
- People rise to a challenge, if it is given.
- A person's loyalty is a function of how he feels he is appreciated.
- Success depends on controlling your environment.
- Dedication is wanting your thing to happen more than *they* want it to happen.
- A person's self-esteem is his most important possession. Don't destroy it.
- Most major jobs can be broken down into several manageable tasks.
- If something is inevitable, acknowledge it and use it to your best advantage.
- Volunteers don't work for money — they work for good feelings.
- If you don't ask the right questions, you won't get the right answers.
- Volunteers are more committed to tasks they have helped develop
- Learn from your mistakes, and keep useful records for your successor.
- Time invested in planning pays off in the end.
- What you feel is not always apparent to others.
- Communication and understanding take effort.
- Prevention is planned anticipation.
- If a worker does not understand *why* he is doing something, he probably won't do it very well.
- Always show more concern for the people than the task. They get the job done for you.
- Creative ideas flourish in a free and open environment.
- Build on the past; don't be tied to it.
- Change is the very thing we *can* count on; are you preparing to deal with it?
- The future will be very different from the past, like it or not.
- If you don't invest time in doing it *right* now, when will you have time to do it over?
- Are you helping those around you to grow and become future leaders?
- Cultivate a positive attitude in yourself and co-workers, if you expect positive results.

LEADERSHIP DEVELOPMENT

Unless you develop the leadership potential within those with whom you work, you are destined to working too hard yourself! Everything will need your attention. In your absence things will come to a virtual halt. And, until you develop a competent replacement, you may be cast in your current position indefinitely. It is an engraved invitation for BURNOUT to set in. Here are several suggestions for developing a capable understudy.

1. Keep your assistant thoroughly posted on your plans and the progress of these plans.
2. Teach him to get into the habit of giving you frequent progress reports.
3. Provide opportunity for him to think for himself. Ask that he bring you possible solutions to any problems he encounters.
4. Place responsibility on him gradually, adding one new assignment at a time.
5. Build up his sense of responsibility. Let him be completely responsible for specific tasks. If he suggests a method as good as yours ... use it.
6. Hold him accountable for his responsibilities ... and make your expectations clear.
7. Make him feel free to ask for new responsibilities. Show that you are anxious for him to develop.
8. Back him up. Give your support publicly, and if it is necessary to criticize, do so privately.
9. Teach him to admit his mistakes promptly. Let him know you want to hear about them from him, before they lead to other problems.
10. Help him learn to take criticism constructively. Let him know you speak of these issues only because you care, about him and the quality of the job he does.

CHARACTERISTICS OF ORGANIZATIONS CAPABLE OF OUTSTANDING PERFORMANCE

Organizations that succeed year after year are those that have a unifying philosophy of self-determination and high hope. They *believe* in their ability to determine their own destiny. They do not cower in the face of obstacles such as a poor economy, too few volunteers, unemployment, etc

With successful organizations there is a sense of purpose to all action and this creates a sense of identity among the staff and volunteers. Each feels he is a critical part of an integrated whole. The organizational purpose is an extension of individual purpose and this allows for the satisfaction of feelings of self-worth.

There is also a commitment to the *people*, not just the *task* at hand. There is concern for the well-being and growth of co-workers. Opportunity is provided for individuals to make a meaningful contribution. The tasks are as important for the development of the individual as for the organization.

The prevailing *attitude* that permeates the group is positive and constructive, and has a tremendous influence on the ultimate success. The climate is set by a strong leader.

Organizations capable of inspired performance seem to have several key elements at work:

- A sense of purpose

- An alignment of individuals around this purpose

- A concern for personal performance and growth

- A commitment to creating a positive working environment

- An effective structure

- A clear line of authority and a strong, sensitive leader

- A level of communication that integrates reason and intuition, allows for creativity, and clarifies expectations

Successful organizations are lead by individuals:

1. Willing to make trade-offs

2. Who work from set goals

3. Who are effective communicators

4. Perceptive and sensitive to the group

5. Good at integrating various interests and priorities

6. Who are creative and adaptable

7. Who provide a positive role model

8. Who acknowledge the efforts of all

6. *Motivation*

"What Makes You Tick?"

*"If you want to gather honey,
don't kick over the beehive."*

Dale Carnegie

A point I have to share is that *you can't motivate others*. We may, if we are very clever, stimulate them to action, but their *motivation* must come from within. Any attempt to motivate others will be met with the same frustration experienced when we attempt to push a string.

In the volunteer world we deal with secondary re-enforcers — elements other than pay checks. Those in business realized some time ago if the pay check is the *only* motivation an employee brings to his job, then quality will likely diminish! As volunteers we can only concern ourselves with feelings: recognition, approval, acceptance and love. These are important in any work situation, but *essential* when we consider a volunteer's job satisfaction. Without them we are rarely motivated to maintain a high standard of performance.

Committeemen invest an element of feeling in their work and a good chairman responds to that investment with empathy and provides meaningful pay-offs. This can be by way of individual recognition or public praise.

On the reverse side, Charles Hobbs reminds us that self-esteem is a person's most treasured possession, and we must seek to handle it with care. A volunteer will move away from an assignment if he is belittled or made to feel inadequate. An employee may stay on under such a circumstance, but he'd hardly be motivated to produce his best work.

LOGIC AND EMOTION

It is a key concept in motivation to remember that when you are dealing with people, you are not dealing with creatures of *logic* but creatures of *emotion* — creatures filled with prejudices and motivated by pride and vanity. With this in mind, it appears obvious that condemning and criticizing them only puts them on the defensive. When this happens, an individual will try every means to justify himself. His *pride* will be wounded, as will his sense of importance, and this arouses resentment.

So, instead of dwelling on drawbacks and weaknesses of volunteers, understand them as people, and try to figure out *why* they do what they do.

According to Freud, how you get your feelings of importance tells a great deal about you, about your character. Some achieve their desire to be great by giving of time, talent or money; others, by ruling over others either positively or negatively. The need to feel significant is an important consideration in stimulating others to *motivate* themselves.

Motivation, as a word, comes from the Latin "movere" — to move toward satisfying a need. It is a response to a stimulus. An example I like is to think in terms of a flower seed. We know it needs light, water and food in order to grow into a healthy flower. We can supply these things, but we can't motivate that seed to utilize them.

Motivation induces action, it provides the *motive*, or inner urge. There must be an inner urge to do things differently, or to do things at all, if there is to be motivation. If you are working with a group of seemingly uncommitted volunteers perhaps it is time to ask a few questions. Consider:

1) What specific goals for achievement do they have? What do you have?
2) Using positive imagery (imagining success), what does their 'success' look like?
   What is your mental picture of success?
3) What are they aware of in terms of things that affect the situation? What are you aware of about the situation?
4) What do they see as the extent of their responsibility to this situation? And yours?
   How do *you* see their responsibility? And yours?
5) What action do they see that they could take to bring about positive results? What do they see you as doing? What actions do *you* see that they could be doing? And you?
6. Are they willing to make a commitment to change or action? Are you?

As a leader the challenge is to inspire interest in positive behavior and to light the way with practical, non-threatening examples of how things could be different and more productive. Be open to change and criticism yourself, as well.

ENVIRONMENT

When you think of co-workers, think of providing an *environment* which will help meet their needs, and this will help in their motivation. This is where an attempt to understand the individual is so important. If, for example, you work with a person who continually offers his services but never completes the task, this behavior affects your entire group. When you ask yourself why he does this, you may begin to realize he simply needs recognition. Can you create an environment where he can receive recognition for positive behavior?

However, it has been determined that removing causes for dissatisfaction, which relate primarily to environmental conditions, does not guarantee future satisfaction. Satisfaction is more than the absence of irritation. Satisfaction is tied to factors intrinsic to the job, the job content.

SATISFACTION (Job Content)	DISSATISFACTION (Job Environment)
1. Sense of achievement	1. Agency policies (if disagreeable)
2. Recognition	2. Relationship with supervisor (if negative)
3. Job itself	3. Working condition (if poor)
4. Responsibility	4. Relationship with co-workers (if tense)
5. Advancement	5. Little recognition for effort

ORIENTATION

Early orientation of new members can greatly influence later enthusiasm within your group. Preplanning a clear-cut set of objectives, for what you hope to accomplish and within what time period, can assure you a larger percentage of happy members in years to come.

First, be sure to describe what is expected of the new member and show how he can develop and grow as a result of his experiences with your organization.

Second, help him to understand the policies of the group and its primary reason for being, as well as how he can be a worthwhile addition to the group.

Third, and perhaps most importantly, seek to make your new member feel welcome and a part of the group as a whole. If he is anxious to become active immediately, help to find an opportunity suited to his talents.

MOTIVATION AND MANAGEMENT

Richard Anderson, in *Motivation — the Master Key*, refers to a manager's "motivation quotient" — which results from two facts: first, your attitude, and second, your management methods.

Community leaders need to begin to see themselves as managers of sorts and to set out to acquire many of the useful tools applied in business. One such point is "give co-workers more personal attention than job attention once they know what they're doing". This is where I refer you to some of the team building ideas. Become sensitive to your fellow-workers

There are 3 basic methods for stimulating people to action. First, you can drive them by unrelenting pressure; second, you can inspire them to give their all for you as their leader (this works effectively only for the charismatic leader); third, you can stimulate them to develop their own capabilities and perform to their own satisfaction. The manager can inspire motivation. He cannot *impose* it.

"Reasons may be compelling, but the way people *feel* affects their conduct more than the way they think."

Constructive criticism must be considered routine, and, as suggested in the Management by Objectives section, each task *should* be evaluated upon conclusion, if not periodically during the process. Members should expect help along the way, not a "put down" at the end. Remember, your criticism always should be of the action, not the individual. *What* concerning the plan or approach didn't work? Don't be personal. This system is designed to alleviate personality conflicts.

Equally important, recognize outstanding performance. Reward real workers publicly, and when possible tangibly, even if it is just with a certificate. Make it a practice to recognize achievement. It's very encouraging.

If you expect people to act on what you say, your own conduct must show that you believe it. You must also communicate that you believe in them and give them adequate tools and explanations to handle the assignment.

Keep in mind that your actions speak louder than words. If you truly want to convey one message, then your own behavior must not be in conflict with your words. You can't ask for dependability and follow-through from your committee members if you yourself perpetually fail to come through or produce as promised.

CLARIFYING EXPECTATIONS

Parent study classes teach that a child will become what you accuse him of being. Tell a child he is lazy, and he will prove you right. Tell him he is thoughtful, and he will prove this to be true. So it is with committee people. They behave pretty much as you expect them to.

If you let people know you are counting on them, and if you demonstrate this confidence by giving them opportunity, the few disappointments you have will be abundantly balanced by the many bonuses of surprising achievement ... If you want to draw out the best in people, you must look for it.

Knowing *why* the behavior exists gives you clues as to how to deal with a problem. Your next step might be to simply try to come up with ways to meet this person's need for recognition, and in doing so, you serve the group as well.

MOTIVATION QUESTIONS

Periodically it might be useful for you to present an opportunity for your members to express *why* they belong to your group. Do you know? It may seem obvious, but then again, it may produce surprises. You could give each of your members 5 index cards at a meeting and have them fill out one, in answer to each of the following questions:

1. Why did you join this group?
2. Are you finding what you hoped to find?
3 How satisfying do you find this experience?
4. Why do you continue to belong?
5. How could the group be better for you?

Then, recording on a large flip chart (see Interaction Recording), report out — tallying the most frequently-mentioned answers. From here you can begin to compare actual experience to members' expectations and then work on ideas for things you might do to make the group more satisfying to most members.

Obviously, this is an effective tool only when applied to small groups (fewer than 30), or when done in committee, as it is important that everyone be able to see the chart.

FEELINGS PEOPLE HAVE ABOUT GROUPS

The following is a list of fairly universally accepted feelings people have about groups. People want:

1. To be free
2. To work through a democracy
3. To find diversity more than conformity
4. To be effective
5. To grow in a feeling of value

When you let others express their hopes and expectations, you increase communication, understanding and the likelihood of a commitment to the very things you need. Consult your co-workers and show respect for their advice. To get things done, set up a challenge and provide a chance for self-expression and success. "Bottoms up is the bottom line." Let changes begin with those who will be most affected by the decisions.

Instead of handing out edicts and orders, you might have more success if you present your wishes as questions and let the committee answer them. This *shares* the responsibility for decision-making, establishes the challenge and provides an opportunity to assure understanding. Most people can't be *sold*, you have to let them *buy*.

The only way we can get volunteers to do anything is by giving them what they want. Therefore, understanding your co-workers is of great importance. Carnegie uses an example of being very fond of strawberries and cream, also of fishing. When he fishes, he doesn't use strawberries as a lure — just because *he* likes strawberries. He motivates the fish with what *they* want — worms! To quote Lloyd George, "BAIT THE HOOK TO SUIT THE FISH."

Remember, you can make more friends in 2 weeks by being interested in others than you can in 2 years trying to get others interested in you. Always make the other person feel important, and in any confrontation, always let the other "save face". If you have your way but lose all of your people or their backing — what will you really have to show for your effort?

Also, it is always easier to listen to unpleasant things after we've heard some praise of our good points. If you must find fault, spend a little time on some *good* aspect of the issue before you get to the *bad*.

We all know we are only producing a small portion of what we are capable in the best of circumstances. When we find ourselves in situations of conflict and frustration, we will produce even less. And, on the more positive side, with inspiration and challenge, we can produce beyond anyone's expectations.

Any activity which stimulates (and that's the key word) a volunteer's natural drive will always inspire greater imagination, resourcefulness and commitment. It's up to the chairmen, the leaders, to cultivate the best in their committee members by controlling the atmosphere of the meetings and applying the talents of the members. Ultimately HOW you do what you do is just as important as WHAT you do.

CONSIDERATIONS FOR ADMINISTRATORS

The Center for Creative Management cites 5 important points for their administrators:

1. Create an environment where each person finds the work for which he is best suited and wants most to do.
2. Give people the tools they need to do their jobs.
3. Challenge them to do their best while giving them the opportunity to do it.
4. Reward them equitably for their efforts.
5. Offer them an opportunity to learn, to grow and to advance.

Regrettably, we are not always in a position to select the people we'd most like for our committees — but when *we* are being asked to serve, we should give considerable thought to the requirements of the position. Will the job suit our talents? You'll be motivated to achieve your best if the job suits your interests and skills.

This handbook is about how *you* can get the most out of being a volunteer. As a chairman you need to remember you can't stimulate others to do their best for you if they don't bring enthusiasm to the challenge. If you are a committee person, you will only be motivated to produce if you sincerely want to become involved — not to please someone else, or because you should, or because no one else will if you don't. Your motivation must be to express yourself and use your talents — as Carl Rogers says — to "self-actualize".

As chairman, you wouldn't want to assign Introverted Ida to the task of selling ads for your program, and relegate Gregarious Glenda to address envelopes. As a committee person when asked to work on a project, consider all the options and offer your assistance in the area most suited to your needs, your talents and your schedule. That's not selfish — that makes sense! It guarantees your interest and commitment. There always will be jobs that seem just awful to you that others would enjoy.

MATCHING SKILLS WITH JOBS

Matching People's Skills to Their Jobs is Vital. Many organizations have nominating committees. These can be treacherous assignments. It is possible they will be expected to talk others into doing things. But this needn't be the case.

A really good nominating committee has access to information about each of the members of the organization, preferably provided by the members themselves through a questionnaire. If people are given the opportunity to indicate relevant experience as well as areas of interest, the matching of people to jobs of their preference will practically guarantee motivation and greatly increase the chances of success for a project.

What you may not realize is that it is important to define the jobs. It is important that the volunteer understand what is expected of him, how long he has to do the job and how much help he'll get. It is also helpful to note what skills are required — and what skills are apt to be acquired.

The selection of a group's Board is probably of greatest importance. With a wise choice of key people, you are more fully assured of the quality of the second string. If your Board is made up of committee chairmen, each should be allowed, where possible, to seek a committee of people he works well with and who will complement him in personality, skill and interest.

It is important to remember that if the whole committee is of like interests, talents and attitudes, little of great value is apt to be accomplished. On the other hand, if the group is too varied, it could become so divisive as to destroy itself. When there are common values, the group will work well on mutually agreed upon goals, with members stimulating and challenging one another — because there is no tension or pressure to compete. They want instead to complement the other. There will be *cooperation* because the group realizes that they will gain from the success of one another.

I read once about a business that rewarded its managers for their loyalty with little regard for leadership qualities. It is appropriate to provide advancement for loyal workers — but there are better ways to reward loyal team members than to promote them beyond their qualifications. Isn't that what we've come to know as "The Peter Principle"? When this happens, the members frequently become frustrated and dissatisfied and too often verbal in their complaints.

Businessmen are beginning to learn that craftsmen need not be promoted to supervisor when what they do best requires different skills. We as volunteers can come to understand ourselves so well that we'll know better than to accept a promotion for the glory of the title, and to stick to the things we've come to do best, or take advantage of training to gain new skills.

This is not to say you shouldn't move beyond your "comfort zone" — rather, have the sense not to do so until you've acquired the needed skills for the task. There are conferences and workshops offered all the time in most large cities where it is possible to gain new skills which will help qualify you for new challenges. Isn't that what we really want? — not to give people jobs because they need them or for the experience, but to give them opportunities to become skilled in varied areas so they become *qualified* to be considered for new positions.

If you know what positions you'd like to hold, try to determine what skills are needed to do the job well and set about achieving them. Then let the powers that be know that you'd like to be considered for the position and that you've gone out of your way to prepare for the challenge.

A really successful organization selects people on the basis of their capabilities, rather than seniority. We need to move away from the idea that our most senior members ought to be president. When people begin to be recognized for their performance and capabilities, others become motivated to expand their opportunities. Incentive is destroyed if a few are always given the key positions.

Perhaps we need to talk a bit about membership in general and how we motivate people to join in the cause that we think is so worthwhile. Too often people are recruited simply because they have the time or a secondary interest, any warm body. This tends to produce an organization top heavy with numbers, a small percentage of whom really care about giving their all.

Beyond the problems of great numbers joining with little real interest — you can also risk having more people than you actually need, and even if they were highly motivated when they signed up, that motivation will diminish rapidly if they aren't given frequent opportunities to make important contributions to the cause. There always will be those who want to say they belong and to appear on the roster and really want to do nothing except pay dues — but we need to recognize those who joined for other reasons and work to maintain a high degree of satisfaction with their association.

I have resigned from groups, not because I no longer believed their cause was good, but because I had changed. My needs had changed, and my goals had changed. And, as I looked at the prospect of meeting and fulfilling these needs, I realized that I wasn't likely to, through these groups, — so it was time to move on. But this requires considerable introspection and coming to grips with who you are and what you need, to be happy and fulfilled.

Let's begin to be more aware of the needs of our members, to listen to their viewpoints, to create an environment which will inspire and challenge, and to provide training opportunities that assure growth and future leadership.

NEEDS OF VOLUNTEERS

By Dr. J. Donald Phillips, Chancellor Emeritus, Hillsdale College, Hillsdale, Michigan (used with permission)

If my best efforts are desired, my leader will know that, as a volunteer, I need . . .

1. To be given *Confidence:*
   To feel that I'm trusted in work assigned to me.
   To be told results desired but not "How to do it".

2. To be given *Recognition* when earned:
   To have my efforts, ideas and work acknowledged.
   To be known, understood and to have concern shown for me as an individual.

3. To have *Delegation* follow accepted guidelines:
   To have reasons for a task explained clearly.
   To have accountabilities clearly prescribed.

4. To get *Feedback* — and be asked for my thoughts and ideas:
   To have one-to-one sessions with leveling on "How am I doing?" (My progress?)
   To be informed on the progress of my organization.
   To find progress toward *my* personal goals.

5. To be *Involved:*
   To be allowed to share in decisions that affect me — as often and as much as possible.
   To be kept "in" on all appropriate information.
   To have opportunities for fair hearings.
   To feel free to ask questions without intimidation.

6. To gain a personal *Sense of Belonging:*
   (see all other items)

7. To be *Challenged* — to be given opportunity:
   To create, discover, compete.
   To have changes in tasks for new challenges and satisfactions.

8. To find *Relevance* — to know:
   "Why?" "Why me?" "Why at this time?" "Why important?"
   Whether I may be contributing to something larger than self, and that goals make sense to *me.*

9. To gain *Increasing Understanding:*
   Of SELF, of Supervisors, of Organization (philosophy, policies, procedures).
   By having opportunities to bounce myself against more Challenges, People, Things.

10. To develop *Confidence* in my Superior, I'd like to see:
    Constancy in method of operation.
    Enthusiasm, a good example, fairness, ability, and above all,
        integrity.

"Your greatest opportunity is to match people with the routines they enjoy."

CONSENSUS

Group consensus inspires motivation because the members feel their input has been acknowledged — they've had a say in how things will be. On appropriate levels it is wise to seek the feelings and opinions of those who will be affected by decisions. This doesn't mean to open any whole topic for debate, but on a committee level to come to an agreement on several possible options. Work from the general, to a specific committee-recommended proposal.

We need to speak briefly about environment again when we're talking about motivation because some situations simply will not stimulate workers to creative participation. Many committee meetings, by necessity, are held in homes. When this is necessary, try to clear the surroundings of distractions — arrange for a neighbor to watch your preschooler and discourage others from bringing their children. Every distraction is a drawback to a successful meeting.

I've participated in Girl Scout Leader Trainings and discovered "cooperative sitters". This is a great idea. A sitter is hired to be on the premises, usually a church, *in another room.* Each leader pays her in accordance with the number of children she brings. The little ones have a wonderful time, and they know mom is nearby. There are other children to play with, and it alleviates the problem of *finding* a sitter. It's a windfall to the sitter who would ordinarily have just one paying customer.

Speaking of Girl Scouts, the girls themselves can often be hired to sit for such things as P.T.A. meetings. Their services can be used as a fund raiser for their troop, or, without pay, as a community service. Not having children in attendance can add greatly to the motivation of the group.

A manager's stock in trade is people. The material resources are made vital by the actions of people, and the manager is the inspiration to these people. The same is true in the volunteer world. Every chairman is dependent upon his committee to allocate time and resources in a manner productive to the cause.

Finally, volunteers need *identity,* and they will do something to achieve this feeling. It is up to the chairman to help each achieve it in a positive, productive manner, remembering that all behavior is rooted in the need structure of the individual.

Satisfaction of our need for self-esteem leads to a feeling of self-confidence, worth, strength, capability, and adequacy. To cultivate this in others we must recognize every opportunity to build up this feeling. By doing this, our coworkers tackle their assignments with a greater feeling of usefulness. The end result is that they are challenged to capacity and their efforts reflect well on us, as chairmen.

HIGH ACHIEVEMENT NEEDS

*Based on material by Kolb, Rubin & McIntyre in *Organizational Psychology, an Experimental Approach,* 1979

People with high achievement needs tend to want:

A. Immediate, concrete feedback, to know as soon as possible how well they are doing so they can adjust their performance to meet their personal needs and goals and those of the organization.

B. Moderate risk-taking situations where there is a personal challenge, but not one left to fate. They like situations where they can be assured of success as long as they are doing their best.

C. Personal responsibility for their own success or failure. When they fail at a task they want to know why, not be given an excuse. They learn from evaluating past performance so as not to repeat their mistakes.

D. Work that is challenging and is structured so as to provide feedback on an on-going basis.

E. An opportunity to develop positive relationships with others while dealing with challenging work.

F. Latitude to make decisions about the process of the work.

To inspire motivation within others be supportive, clarify *your* expectations, give constructive, on-going feedback, and ask opinions. Involve people from the bottom up. Allow those affected by the decisions to be a part of the decision-making process. Offer opportunity for growth and be prepared to enlarge both the scope of individual jobs and the responsibility as well.

People want to be appreciated and to know that what they do is significant. Most would like increased challenges and responsibilities. They need the encouragement and assurance of someone they admire, and they need high expectations. Expect the best and you are more apt to get the best. Set the stage for enthusiasm and success and you will nurture it in others. Provide a fertile environment in which those around you may grow. Be a mentor. Share your skills and talents. Be an inspiration to others!

MOTIVATION FACTORS

Motivating others involves an awareness of their:

- Values
- Needs
- Interests
- Self concept

1. VALUES influence personal decisions because they are tied to the individual's priority system. Those who value their *time* will fall to the wayside if they find meetings to be a waste of their time. Members who value *social interaction* may drop out if they find meetings are too structured and business-like.
2. NEEDS are those inner urges that cause us to act. When things are comfortable there is no *need* to look for change or alternatives. However, if things are stressful members move to change things. They may move 'out' to get away, or 'up' because there is a creative, challenging stress at work.
3. INTERESTS will differ from one member to another, and from one group to another. Though one common cause may bring members together, individual skills and talents account for the activity, within this frame, which will interest each.
4. SELF-CONCEPT is significant in that the appeal of the group or specific task hinges, to a great extent, on how the individual feels he fits into this picture, whether he is 'up' to it or even 'above' it. To motivate (stimulate) an individual the activity must be congruent with the person's self-concept.

DEFENSE MECHANISMS

Many times we hide our feelings by using defenses. Each defense serves to avoid naming the feeling we are experiencing. The use of these may keep us from being known, even to ourselves. To expose the real feelings it takes honest inquiry into *why* the individual is demonstrating the particular response. It always relates to the pursuit of a need — and often is founded in the attempt to maintain our self-image. (It may be very disconcerting to discover we are not who we'd like to think we are.) It can make people uncomfortable to confront the causes of their behavior — but it is the only way to intercept non-constructive behavior (such as defense mechanisms represent).

Defenses Which We All Use to Some Extent Are:

Rationalizing

Justifying

Projecting

Blaming, accusing

Judging, moralizing

Intellectualizing

Analyzing

Exclaiming

Theorizing

Generalizing

Quibbling

Questioning

Switching subjects

Denying

Being superior or arrogant

Agreeing

Displaying anger

Minimizing

Evading, dodging

Defying

Attacking

Withdrawing

Being silent

Verbalizing, talking

Threatening

Frowning

Glaring

Staring

Joking, laughing

Complying

VOLUNTEER INTEREST

The following points are made to help you recognize why volunteers lose interest, as well as factors which encourage them to remain committed. Reasons for losing interest include:

WHY VOLUNTEERS LOSE INTEREST
1. Discrepancies between their expectations in membership or task, and the reality of the situation
2. No feeling of making a difference — no praise or reward
3. Too routine, no variety
4. Lack of support from co-workers
5. Little prestige related to the task or group
6. No chance for personal growth
7. No chance to meet personal needs
8. Too little chance to demonstrate initiative or creativity
9. Tension among co-workers

WHY VOLUNTEERS REMAIN COMMITTED
There are also identifiable reasons why people remain committed. These include:
1. They feel appreciated
2. They can see their presence does make a difference
3. There is a chance for advancement
4. There is opportunity for personal growth
5. They receive private and public recognition
6. They feel capable of handling the tasks offered
7. There is a sense of belonging and teamwork among co-workers
8. They are involved in the administrative process, like problem-solving, decision-making and objective-setting
9. They recognize that something significant is happening because the group exists
10. Their personal needs are being met

FACTORS THAT MOTIVATE ME

The check list below is intended as an assessment tool for individual volunteers.

Indicate 5 items from the list below that you feel are the most important in motivating you.

_____ I enjoy it; it is interesting
_____ Others are doing it
_____ It leads to recognition from others
_____ I have the skill to do it
_____ I feel the task is important
_____ It is easy
_____ I feel trusted and respected in it
_____ I have the opportunity to do a good job
_____ I am expected to do it
_____ I have a chance to help with the planning
_____ I get along well with others at the task
_____ I have a good supervisor or leader
_____ I have a large amount of freedom doing it
_____ I have the opportunity to take responsibility
_____ I have the opportunity to grow and develop on the job
_____ I have the opportunity to meet others
_____ I have the opportunity to make career contacts
_____ I can do most of the work at home
_____ There is a routine I can count on
_____ (Other)

Now, when offered a volunteer challenge, consider first if the position offers the opportunity for satisfaction, in keeping with what you have listed as important.

BASIC PSYCHOLOGICAL NEEDS

The following needs are basic to the psychological development and growth of an individual. Volunteer leaders would do well to periodically assess how well they are doing in creating an environment which will satisfy these basic needs.

1. *Acceptance:* The need to feel that others' attitudes toward one are positive

2. *Achievement:* The need to acquire, gain, receive, win or strive to accomplish

3. *Affection:* The need to be loved, cherished, emotionally wanted for one's own sake

4. *Approval:* The need to have others' behavior toward one indicate that one is a satisfactory person

5. *Belonging:* The need to feel a part of a group or institution

6. *Conformity:* The need to be like others, to avoid marked departure from the mode

7. *Dependence:* The need to have to ask for or depend on others for emotional support

8. *Independence:* The need to do things free from external control by friends, family, associates or others

9. *Mastery-dominance:* The need to control, to be in power, to lead, to manage

10. *Recognition:* The need to be noticed, to become known

11. *Self-realization:* The need to function at one's ability level

12. *To be understood:* The need to feel you have rapport with parents, relatives and friends

MASLOW'S HIERARCHY OF NEEDS

adapted from *Motivation & Personality* A. H. Maslow, Harper, New York, 1954,

(used with permission)

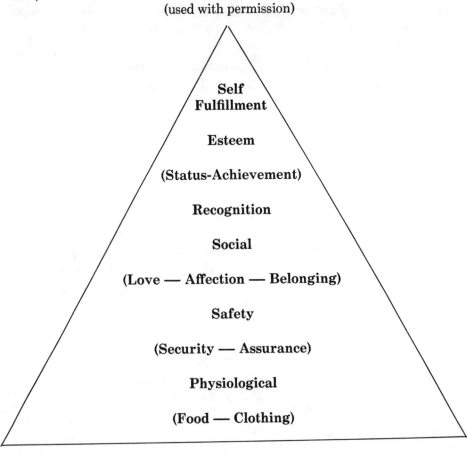

An individual is not motivated to satisfy needs on any level without having the needs on all levels below them satisfied. Once the lower level needs are satisfied, they no longer serve as motivators.

7. Communication

"Am I Getting Through?"

To Communicate: "To impart to another, to make known" WEBSTERS. To truly communicate, understanding must take place.

I know that you believe
you understand what you
think I said

but . . .

I am not sure you realize
that what you heard is
not what I meant.

Communication, by definition, involves at least two individuals, the sender and the receiver. As a sender your message is filtered through assumptions about what you want to share and attitudes about the message itself. As a receiver what is *heard* is filtered through your own set of priorities. You are, at least to some degree, selective in your attention.

To a greater or lesser extent (as determined by the situation and relationship) we are willing and able to communicate only what we perceive. Our "truth" is based on what we are aware of, but our "behavior" is affected by our *unconscious* beliefs as well. These are all the things you choose not to know about — generally because self-discovery can be disheartening.

Anger is one thing that becomes displaced because of unconscious needs and wants. A defensive response may come out when an individual fears that the other person is probably right. The expressed anger may not relate to the current situation or conversation.

Behavior in one setting can be affected by feelings in another. And, the *words* communicated in any situation carry only part of the message — more spontaneous and accurate is the *body language*. Look for this, learn to read it.

EFFECTIVE COMMUNICATION

For *effective communication* to take place it must be OK to tell the truth, the whole truth, to clarify feelings, and to work at dispelling misconceptions. This means sharing good things as well as things felt to be negative. If there is a communication problem work on WHY (there is a problem) — before you work on communication skills (such as "I messages" and "feedback").

Good communication depends first on a healthy, trusting relationship. When people are reluctant to share the truth, it is because they don't have confidence in their own ability to handle the response ... the risk is felt to be too great. But, by not telling the truth, you build a barrier — you have no *connection* with the other, and thus no closeness. Honesty brings people closer, because it removes barriers. To achieve this you may need to endure some periods of high emotion — and that can be frightening as well as uncomfortable.

Circumstances are only circumstances. They don't arrive evaluated. It is the *response* by each person which affects behavior. This response will depend on your belief and perception of the situation *and* your feelings about yourself in the relationship. If there is a conflict it may be that you each *perceive* the situation differently. You must clarify your perceptions of the reality before you can work on your feelings and responses toward it.

Taking responsibility for your feelings and responses demonstrates that you feel you have power to change the things that happen to you. These feelings allow you to be more open and to communicate more honestly.

Feelings that affect honest communications include:

1) Sense of significance (how much you feel a part of things)
2) Sense of control (how you 'fit', how you feel about your competence level in the heirarchy)
3) Sense of openness (how well-liked you feel)

If you communicate in a descriptive rather than evaluative way, the listener's response will be less defensive. It is also helpful to be specific rather than general in your comments. As you communicate, consider the needs of your listener and avoid comments directed at behavior or circumstances over which the listener has no control.

Feedback is a way of giving help when an individual wants to learn how well his behavior and message match his intentions. If you're not getting feedback, chances are you're not communicating.

Feedback is most useful when the listener has asked for your feelings — avoid *imposing* comments on a non-receptive ear. Also important in successful communication is *timing* . The listener must be ready to hear your comments.

Continually check with the listener to assure that your messages are being accurately received. Ask for feedback, and seek to rephrase what you are hearing in order to determine clarity.

TECHNIQUES FOR IMPROVING PERSON-TO-PERSON COMMUNICATION

The following are key points to remember in person-to-person communication:

1. Draw out. Ask questions that require the other person to give structure to his answer. Probe fully for each explanation. Or, stop talking — this allows the other person to complete his thoughts more fully. Finally, never interrupt. This frustrates any effort to communicate.

2. Interpret back. Offer your interpretation of what you've heard, in order to test for accuracy.

3. Present one idea at a time. People have a short attention span. To bombard your listener with several ideas at one time is to assure that at least some will not be remembered.

4. Get acceptance of one idea before moving on to the next. Before moving to a second idea elicit from your listener some assurance that your first idea has been understood.

5. Be explicit. Say what you mean as precisely as possible. Generalities become ambiguous.

6) *Be responsive to emotions* — convey an encouraging expression, show sympathy, be reassuring and share praise.

7) *Share your ideas and feelings* — set a trusting example.

8) *Precede any negative comments with 2 points of praise* — establish an accepting attitude in the listener so he will be open and receptive to your words.

9) *Work consciously on tact* — and think of how you would respond if the tables were turned.

10) *Place yourself in the other's position* — and choose words that aren't put-downs or that imply anything negative about this listener that you did not intend. Your own good intentions are not enough.

I've suggested, at several points, that non-verbal communication also carries profound messages. It is body language which conveys the emotional message. It is partly instinctive and partly learned. Be aware that these messages are being transmitted. Many times they are far more accurate than the verbal ones.

Stimulating the other person to listen is as important as transmitting ideas. The techniques for inspiring motivation have more to do with feelings and emotions than with intellect. Try to:

- Be responsive to emotions. Expressions of feelings are woven into the fabric of communication, and they must be acknowledged through sympathizing, reassuring, praising and through encouraging expressions.
- Give of yourself. When you share your ideas and feelings with another, he is motivated to reciprocate. Develop mutual trust.

Repetitive Irritants

Repetitive irritants automatically turn people off. Effort should be made to eliminate these from your conversations. Remember, we don't always see our own faults — but we can learn to notice. Others may not tell you that you are doing these things — in words, but their body language behavioral response may shout at you.

Examples:

- Talking to a person, through someone else
- Telling people, "don't worry"
- Topping everyone else's story
- Doing all the talking, dominating
- Calling across the room, or interrupting
- Not speaking up when appropriate, but complaining later
- Changing the subject midstream
- Putting someone down — especially in front of others
- Taking your anger out on an innocent bystander
- Giving people the runaround, instead of straight answers . . . these are repetitive irritants.

It doesn't matter how your message sounds to you. How does it sound to your listener? In communicating successfully, we must begin with a *content* message, stating briefly what we want to say; then elaborate to clarify; and finally restate our key points. "Whole-part-whole". Briefly state your whole message (tell them what you're going to tell them); then in a more detailed manner, give the listeners each of the parts (tell them); and conclude with a summary of the whole again (tell them what you told them).

We need also to consult and review the Management by Objectives section of this book when we talk about communicating. We cannot succeed in a project or in relaying a message if we don't clearly define our objectives. Make clear what you are trying to do or say.

Key points to remember include giving co-workers all the information they need to proceed, but don't swamp them with unneeded information. Communication is a two-way process. It is important to solicit feedback periodically to confirm that your message is being heard accurately.

As an effective communicator you must:

1) Speak clearly and loud enough
2) Speak in an organized manner in a logical sequence
3) Use clarifying inflection and precise words
4) Speak from the diaphragm
5) Look at your listener
6) Speak from assurance or acknowledge that your words represent opinion
7) Keep your emotions in check — express them in words ("that really makes me angry")
8) Be responsive to the needs and questions of others
9) Select words that have meaning to the listener
10) Listen to yourself and be sure you are saying what you mean

BARRIERS TO GOOD COMMUNICATION

Even if you are conscious of, and careful about, each of the above points there are still many factors which complicate good communication. These can be considered barriers to good communication.

1) Cultural differences
2) Environmental conditions
3) Differences in frame of reference
4) Poor articulation
5) Thinking faster than we can speak
6) Evaluation of the concepts, instead of listening for full meaning and implication
7) Failure to determine from the other how accurately you are being heard
8) The tendency to proceed without seeking feedback from the listener

Again, feedback remains an essential element in effective communication. The following points are made to help guide you in giving feedback.

CRITERIA FOR EFFECTIVE FEEDBACK

1) It is descriptive rather than evaluative
2) It is specific not general
3) It takes into account the needs of both the speaker and the receiver
4) It focuses only on behavior which can be changed
5) Clarification is sought
6) It is solicited, rather than imposed
7) It is well timed
8) It is based on a sincere interest in the other persons' perceptions
9) Avoid asking "why" (other phrasing is more useful)
10) Focus on observations rather than references
11) Seek to consider elements in terms of more or less — not either/or
12) Explore alternatives rather than answers or solutions

An effective way to communicate is to develop your thoughts with sentences which include each of the following points:

Formulating a complete thought:

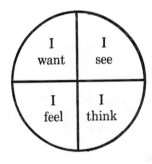

Develop a sentence that includes each point.

"I *see* (Documentation w/o judgment) . . .,
I *think* — you are (not) . . .,
I *feel* . . ., and,
I *want* . . . (be specific)
For example, "I *see* you have missed 5 of the last 6 meetings. I *think* we need to talk about this. I *feel* you may not really be interested in our committee. I *want* you to consider whether you'd like to resign."

Communication is not a destination — it is a journey. The map is not the territory, the model is not the experience, the menu is not the food. We must *encode* our ideas to communicate them to others. The words we choose may have a different meaning to the listener.

SERIAL COMMUNICATION

Based on material by Marty Squire, consultant
(used with permission)

Serial communication takes place when a message goes through several senders before it reaches its final destination. It is both essential and inevitable in organizations. At the same time it is very susceptible to distortion and disruption. Frequently, some of the content is omitted or added to in retelling.

- Details of varying importance to the transmitter become changed or dropped entirely.

- Details which remain are highlighted and take on increasing importance.

- Details become modified to conform to the transmitter's attitudes, experience, knowledge or to what he expected to hear.

- Details are added to or exaggerated, to embellish or liven up the description.

- Order of events becomes rearranged. Things are said to have happened in an order that might be expected or that seems more logical and probable to the transmitter.

- Statements that were orginally tentative or qualified become facts as do inferences and assumptions.

- Ambiguous or unclear details are adapted to make them seem more plausible or reasonable to the transmitter.

Why do these things happen? In general, as the message is passed along, each transmitter wants to make it as simple, sensible and usually as pleasant and painless as possible. Under some circumstances, however, some transmitters have hidden motives which lead them to make messages bigger and worse! The point to remember about serial communication is that a message almost never reaches the final listener in its original form. Each transmitter along the way has not just reproduced the original but has re-created it according to his needs, tastes or beliefs.

What can be done to reduce the distortion?

- Make the message both written and oral if accuracy is required.

- Keep the message as short as possible with a minimum number of separate details in it.

- Keep the original message sensible and orderly and as free of ambiguities as possible.

- Ask the listener to repeat it to determine accuracy of reception.

- Try to anticipate any difficulties the listener may be having and deal with them.

- Reduce the number of links in the chain.

- If you are the last person in the chain and the information is essential to you, go back to the original source for verification, if possible.

If you ever doubt the distortion caused by serial communication, try the following exercise.

Prepare a single, descriptive paragraph for one individual to read to another. Ask the second individual to *tell* a third person what she heard and ask that person to relay the message to still a fourth. (The latter two hearing the message for the first time). What you will discover is that the last "telling" of the story differs greatly from the original paragraph. Because each listener brought a different bias and perspective to his "hearing", he colored his "telling" accordingly.

LEVELS OF COMMUNICATION: CONTENT AND PROCESS

Communication takes place on two levels — content and process. Listen to voice tones and emphasis in the following and consider how many different things can be meant by changed inflection:

1) *I* never said he stole the money

2) I *never* said he stole the money

3) I never *said* he stole the money

4) I never said *he* stole the money

5) I never said he *stole* the money

6) I never said he stole the *money*

Real communication occurs when we listen with understanding, and this requires that we seek clarification.

ELEMENTS OF COMMUNICATION

When making a presentation or proposal, or planning a training or orientation session — Remember:

— We learn approximately:
1% through taste
2% through touch
4% through smell
10% through hearing
83% through sight

— People generally remember:
10% of what they read
20% of what they hear
30% of what they see
50% of what they hear and see

If your audience retains 50% of what is presented to it, your are a successful communicator.

BASIC WRITING

Volunteer leaders depend on the written word. It is the most used and most effective medium of communication. Writing clearly is essential. The more clearly you write, the better others will understand the subject you are discussing. Many times, a letter, memo or report is not understood by the recipient because it is not written clearly or does not say what the writer actually intended to say.

To make your writing easy for you and your readers, consider these 5 basic steps:

1. *Put an idea into one sentence.* Assuming that you have accomplished the required fact-finding and leg work, write down the essence, gist, idea or theme of what you are going to say. The sentence needn't be fancy, catchy or brilliant. Writing in a simple manner is not always easy. Anyone can write complex sentences that leave the reader to sort out the facts.

2. *Organize your thoughts.* Keep in mind the people who may be influenced by what you are writing. Review your letter, memo or report through the eyes of the reader. Who is he? What is he interested in learning from you? Imagine yourself carrying on a verbal conversation with the reader. This may help you write a message that is clear and to the point. Write as if you were talking.
   Write to express thoughts, not to impress people. Clear thinking is necessary before you ever put a word on paper. Gather your material, consider the order of importance and determine the tone of your material; *then* begin to write.

3. *Make your writing simple.* Start out with something to arouse interest. Don't quote from someone else if you have something to say personally.

4. *Make your writing easy for the reader.* Don't use unnecessary words. The reader may not take the time to hunt for what you are trying to say. Simplicity demands conciseness. Use short, direct, simple statements to cover basic points and state them in a well-organized manner.

If you are inclined to use words such as "and", "but", "however", or "consequently" in the middle of sentences, try putting in a period instead. You will find this adds clarity to what you are saying. Be economical with words.

In business letters and auxiliary communications, avoid timeworn, stilted phrases, such as: "this is to advise", and "thank you in advance".

Several common errors in writing:

Don't use "first annual". If it is a first, it can't be annual.

"Presidents-elect", not "president-elects".

The whole is "comprised" of its parts, not "composed" of its parts.

"Demolish" and "destroy" mean to do away with completely. You can't "partially" demolish or destroy, and it is redundant to write "totally destroyed".

"Ecology" and "environment" are not the same. Ecology is the study of the relationship between organisms and their environment.

"Funeral service" is redundant. A funeral is a service.

People don't "head up" committees; they "head" them.

Speakers "imply". Listeners "infer".

Temperatures go higher or lower, not warmer or cooler.

Redundancies: Easter Sunday (Easter is enough); Jewish Rabbi (just Rabbi); winter months (just winter); incumbent Congressman (just Congressman).

"Unique" — this means one of a kind. Nothing can be "rather unique".

For a test of meaning listen to this: a foreign marketing man once translated back into English a popular phrase which had earlier been translated into his language. The latter became: "Invisible things are insane." The original? "Out of sight, out of mind!" This illustrates the point that often our words are equally as foreign to the listener. Double entendres may be impossible to grasp, such as "They'll eat that up." We should make it a point to say what we mean, as clearly as possible, in terms recognizable to the listener, and, without sarcasm.

Children are apt to grasp only the command in a message, rather than the admonishment "not to". "Don't touch the vase" becomes "touch the vase". As adults we may also fall into this selective hearing.

So much hinges on communication. If we fail to share with those with whom we work:

— what we expect of them

— by what deadline

— in what manner,

we may always be frustrated by pure confusion.

ATTITUDE

There is an ad for a beer that shows two couples dressed to the hilt ready for a banquet. They discover the banquet was the previous night. The group laughs cheerfully, their shoes and ties are shed and the group settles in comfortably at home to enjoy a *banquet* of their own beer. This struck me as a great example of *attitude*. There were at least two options here: to become upset and exasperated because a planned event was missed, which won't change anything; it wouldn't cause the banquet to be held tonight or in the future. What it is likely to do is ruin the atmosphere for all the others. The alternative is to laugh it off, make the most of it and move on.

We *convey* our attitudes and affect the atmosphere by various forms of communication. Body language alone can tell others we are disappointed or excited or angry. We should try to intercept negative feelings before they materialize.

We possess just so much energy, and it strikes me as a great waste to invest it in non-productive discussion about what might have been or should have been. When working with other volunteers, we have no obligation to discipline them for their failures. We need to maintain an agreeable atmosphere and convey an attitude of understanding.

SOME DO'S AND DON'T'S OF FACE-TO-FACE COMMUNICATIONS

Do:

- Learn to express yourself. Practice. If necessary take a speech course.
- Use your personality. Smile! Be pleasant.
- Evaluate your problems. Know why a decision was made and share the logic of this thinking.
- Consider the perspective of your listener. What is his bias, and what will your words mean from his point of view?
- When necessary, rephrase your point to assure clarification.
- Speak with a voice of confidence. Be quiet and cordial.
- Let others express themselves; allow them to differ and give them room to retreat.
- Show understanding and patience with the listener.
- Accept differences of opinions without becoming angry or upset.

- Remember, not everyone is going to agree with you ... be willing to change your position.

Don't:

1. Be bossy
2. Use sarcasm
3. Become angry or pout
4. Take things personally
5. Threaten others
6. Swear
7. Lose your poise
8. Lose your patience
9. Take a position from which you can't deviate or retreat
10. Retreat, unless logical thinking convinces you your thinking was erroneous

JOHARI WINDOW

One of the factors that greatly affects communication is our perception of ourselves. Each of us enters into conversation with a picture of ourselves that we try to maintain and project. The listener brings to this encounter his perception of us, which differs from our own (and in the case of a stranger this opinion is formed in the first four minutes!). The Johari Window explains how this works.

	Known to self	Not known to self
Known to Others	I Free Activity	II Blind Spot
Not Known to Others	III Private, Secret, Hidden	IV Unknown

Quadrant I: Information known to self and known to others
Quadrant II: Information *not* known to self, but known to others
Quandrant III: Information known to self, but *not* known to others
Quandrant IV: Information *not* known to self and *not* known to others

COMMUNICATION QUIZ

	1	3	5
Do you:	Seldom —	Usually —	Always

1. Realize that what you see may differ from what others see?
2. Realize that what people choose to say about a situation is their abbreviated version?
3. Avoid labeling and using demeaning words which destroy anyone's self-esteem?
4. Phrase your thoughts in "I" messsages which describe how you feel about the situation?
5. Avoid terms which imply *black* or *white,* such as *always* or *never?*
6. Recognize that some of your words may be misinterpreted?
7. Acknowledge that your feelings and emotions can affect what you hear, see and say?
8. Seek to clarify your message by asking for a demonstration of understanding?
9. Ask for feedback and clarifications when in doubt about the other person's meaning?
10. Accept correction when it is obvious that you've been wrong?
11. Tune into body language which might indicate misunderstanding?
12. Avoid exaggeration and evaluation and pursue accurate understanding?

60 is a perfect score. Less than 40 indicates that you could use some work in the area of communication skills.

DALE'S CONE OF EXPERIENCE*
Below is a diagram of Dale's Cone.

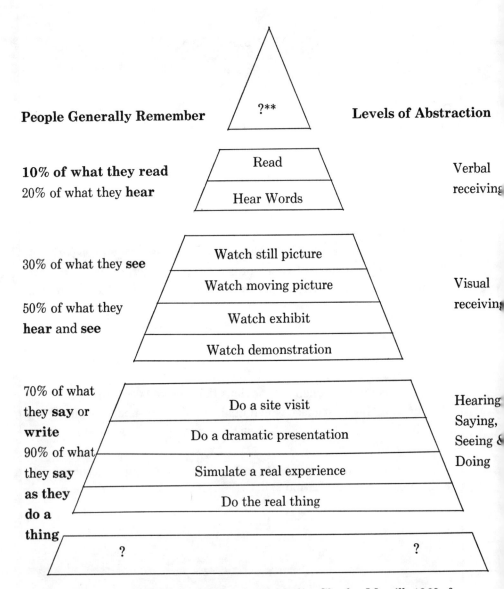

People Generally Remember

?**

Levels of Abstraction

10% of what they read
20% of what they **hear**

Read

Hear Words

Verbal
receiving

30% of what they **see**

Watch still picture

Watch moving picture

Visual
receiving

50% of what they
hear and **see**

Watch exhibit

Watch demonstration

70% of what
they **say** or
write

Do a site visit

Do a dramatic presentation

Hearing
Saying,
Seeing &
Doing

90% of what
they **say**
as they
do a
thing

Simulate a real experience

Do the real thing

?

?

*From Wiman & Mierhenry, *Educational Media,* Charles Merrill, 1969, for
reference to Edgar Dale's "Cone of Experience", used with permission.
**Question marks refer to the unknown.

8. *Listening*

"Do You Hear Me?"

"The reason you don't understand me, Edith, is because I'm talking to youse in English and you're listenin' to me in Dingbat!"
Archie Bunker

It has been said that the need to be listened to is so great that if it were completely absent from one's daily existence, one would probably begin to talk to oneself!

We need responses of all kinds, and one of the most satisfying is being listened to when you want to be heard. Knowing that people care about what you have to say is important to your feeling of self-worth.

Beyond this, it is a comfort to know that your message has been understood. One problem that could arise is that the message sent by the speaker is not always the message received by the listener. This is due in part to the assumptions we live by:

1. Your view of how things are and what is real (what you're really like and what the world is really like)

2. Your value system (what you believe to be *good* or *bad, right* or *wrong* and how things *should* be)

3. How things *could* be and your possibilities for personal growth

Another part of the problem stems from *connotative* difficulties — the fact that different words mean different things to different people, and *denotative* or content messages — having to do with the differences in the meanings of the words themselves.

Dr. Paul Watzlawick has introduced still another area of potential confusion — the *meta level*. A "meta-communication" or meta message is a message about a message: posture, attitude, tone of voice and facial expression (non-verbal language) — all affect communication, and thus our listening.

People whom Maslow describes as "self actualized" (see chapter on motivation) share a number of character traits. One is the acceptance of themselves and others for what they are. However, most of us are in the process of *becoming* and are not fully actualized, and we spend most of our energies on our lower level needs. Preoccupied with meeting these needs, we are unlikely to tune in to the needs of others and really listen.

Our school systems promote reading, and this is certainly an essential skill. However, *listening* is something we are not generally taught ... it is something we must learn. To learn to listen effectively, it is essential to understand the various factors involved in listening.

LISTENING REQUIRES WORKING AT LISTENING AND UNDERSTANDING WHAT THE OTHER PERSON HAS TO SAY.

There are 5 components of good listening:
1. Acceptance (acknowledge that you are listening)
2. Reflection (repeat the speaker's words)
3. Clarification (ask for meaning or further explanation)
4. Interpretation (absorb what has been said and reword it)
5. Summary (tie up what has been said in order to conclude)

Active listening is understanding without judging. It is more than listening to the *content* of the message; it also is trying to *understand* what is behind the content.

Confusion can be avoided if we rely more on a *description* of our feelings. If we make a concerted effort to encourage our committee people to express their feelings about what is happening, we can expect to avoid later trauma, when they surely will find some way to vent any negative feelings.

We must beware lest our feelings may lead us to make incorrect inferences about others. To better understand the feelings of our co-workers, encourage them to describe their feelings with "I" messages: "I feel used", "I feel inadequate for the job", "I feel overlooked". You can send *feedback* and attempt to rephrase what you're hearing to see if you have absorbed the intended meaning. ("You seem upset. How would you have preferred it be handled?")

As a listener your reaction to the speaker can greatly affect communication. It is a bit unfair to say, "She is boring," when you more honestly mean, "*I* find her boring". Your own attitude plays a great part in what you hear.

Of all the ways a listener can encourage openness and a feeling of acceptance, the most important is facial expression. The way you say it, the tone of your voice, etc., accounts for about a third of what the other person perceives. I've thoroughly enjoyed working with one president because she makes my every idea sound like the best thing the group has ever considered, and she does it more with expression, tone and inflection than choice of words. Your facial expression should help communicate that you really want to hear what the other person has to say.

Because our behavior says so much, we should become aware of what kinds of inferences others make from it. Remember, you will not see or hear the same events or words in precisely the same way as anyone else. Differences due to *perception, motivation, expectancies, personal bias* and such, affect your observations and inferences.

MISCONCEPTIONS ABOUT LISTENING

There are a number of misconceptions about good listening. Among these are the idea that ability depends largely on intelligence, and that in learning to read we will automatically learn to listen. A good listener must apply specific skills acquired through training or experience. If these have not been acquired, the ability to understand and retain what is heard will be low . . . this can happen whether people have high or low intelligence.

While some of the skills needed for good reading apply to good listening, the assumpton that one goes with the other is invalid. Listening is a very different activity from reading.

It is easier to concentrate while reading, watching or doing, than while listening. Distractions register more easily, in part because we think so much more quickly than the speaker speaks. This leaves our minds open to process hundreds of words (and other factors) in addition to those we hear, assembling thoughts other than those spoken to us. The average listener remembers only 25% of what was said, and within 8 hours he forgets nearly one half of that! Frequently we forget more in the first few hours than we do in the next 6 months.

The basic problem with listening is that we THINK MUCH FASTER THAN WE TALK, and while we are listening, we must ask our brain to receive words at an extremely slow pace compared with its capabilities. When listening, we still have spare time for *thinking*. The idea is to direct this thinking to the message being received.

To help people listen better show them how to use their spare *thinking time* more effectively. They must learn to direct a maximum amount of thought to the message being received, leaving little time for mental side tracking away from the speaker's message.

FOUR PRODUCTIVE LISTENING ACTIVITIES:

1. Listen ahead of the speaker; prepare for the direction of thought
2. Weigh the evidence of the speaker, but withhold judgment
3. Periodically review and mentally summarize the points
4. Listen between the lines for additional meaning

And, remember, facts are for constructing *ideas* — grouping *ideas* is what good listening is all about, using the *facts* only long enough to understand the ideas that are built from them.

Our listening ability is also affected by our emotions. Refrain from judgmental listening, and be open to new ideas or perspectives.

When possible, write down what you are hearing. Approximately 85% of what comes into the brain is through the eyes, only 11% through the ears. Taking notes can help you to hear with more accuracy. Write down highlights and key points.

Another advantage to writing things down is that it shows the speaker that you truly care about what is being said. Once in writing, it can also be used for confirmation, "this is what I hear you saying, is it what you meant?"

There are many things you can do to become a better listener. Below is a LADDER for successful listening to use as a guide.

LADDER FOR GOOD LISTENING

L   *L*ook at the speaker, show an active interest. (When the eyes are elsewhere so is the mind).

A   *A*sk questions. Closed-end questions, who, what, when, where, reveal specific facts, open-end questions draw the other person out with why and how?

D   *D*on't interrupt! It's as rude to step on ideas as toes.

D   *D*on't change subjects. Interrupting is bad enough, but changing the subject compounds the error.

E   *E*motions. Keep them from interfering with real communication.

R   *R*esponsiveness. Be responsive in demeanor, posture, facial expression and tone of voice.

For total listening, learn to **HEAR:**

H   *H*ave a hearing check, you may not be aware of a slight hearing loss.

E   *E*valuate the evidence of the speaker for concrete support of his ideas.

A   *A*nticipate the point of communication and direction.

R   *R*eview mentally, the key points and summarize what you hear.

DO YOU HEAR ME?

For listening to occur there are four steps: hearing, understanding, evaluating, and reacting. A good listener learns to adapt these steps into basic conversation.

When concern is shown, by the communicator, for the environment in which the conversation takes place, listening will be more effective. Easily 80% of our volunteer activities depend on listening. Understanding, without distortion, determines the success of our various tasks, as well as the feeling we generate in those with whom we work. Time invested in the environment is worth every minute.

Listening is a process of decoding one message and reassembling it in our minds, based on previous knowledge. For this reason it is as important to listen for concepts, as much as for content. And, all words are absorbed through an emotional filter. We tend to turn off what we don't want to hear.

For this reason it is important to 'market' our ideas for our audiences, to think consciously about what they want to hear and how to make our points most palatable.

Thinking, and resistence, drops to a minimum when we are listening to ideas that we have harbored for years or that support our inner feelings. Our mental barriers are dropped and everything is welcomed. The challenge, as a speaker, is to create the kind of environment in which the listener will be receptive to our ideas. As a listener, tune in to your speaker with empathy and you will *hear* more.

BLOCKS TO GOOD LISTENING:

There are at least six factors which inhibit good listening; these include:

- Feeling you must answer or come to a decision about what is presented to you
- Evaluating what is presented to you
- Being hurried and listening on the run
- Hearing only what you want to hear
- Interrupting because *you* have something to say
- Seeing the other person as different from yourself (in terms of group, culture, race or philosophy).

Response styles lie at the heart of effective listening. They can act as facilitators of communication or as inhibitors. Interpersonal communication is a process of give and take. Whenever a person communicates something to you, the way you respond has the potential to direct the course of the ensuing message.

At one time or another one of the following responses may be appropriate, or at least expedient.

- advice-giving
- interpretation
- cross-examination
- reassurance
- paraphrasing

If the purpose of your communication is to share feelings then you need to realize all but the last act as inhibitors. With *paraphrasing* the intention is to find out whether what you heard is what the speaker intended. This response lets the other person know you are sensitive on the *feeling* level.

To be a responsible, successful listener, focus on the other person. Learn to empathize — project yourself into the situation of the other person and experience the sensation believed to be a part of it.

TEN COMMANDMENTS FOR GOOD LISTENING

1. **Stop talking!**
    You cannot listen if you are talking.

2. **Put the speaker at ease.**
    Help him feel that he is free to talk.

3. **Show others that you want to listen.**
    Look and act interested. Don't busy yourself with other things. Listen to understand, rather than to oppose.

4. **Remove distractions.**
    Don't doodle, tap or shuffle papers. Would it be quieter if you shut the door?

5. **Empathize with others.**
    Try to put yourself in the other's place so as to see his point of view.

6. **Be patient.**
    Allow plenty of time. Do not interrupt. Avoid heading for the door.

7. **Hold your temper.**
    An angry person gets the wrong meaning from words.

8. **Go easy on arguments and criticism.**
    This puts others on the defensive. They may "clam up" or become angry. Do not argue, because even if you win, you lose.

9. **Ask questions.**
    This is encouraging and shows you are listening. It helps to develop points further and is essential for clarification.

10. **Stop talking!**
    This is first and last, because all other commandments depend on it. You simply can't be a good listener while you are talking.

LISTENING I.Q.

	1	3	5
Do you —	Seldom,	Usually,	Always

___ 1. Give the speaker your full and undivided attention?

___ 2. Listen for key words and underlying feelings?

___ 3. Avoid prejudging the value of the words until you've heard the speaker out?

___ 4. Wait until the speaker has completed his thought before sharing yours?

___ 5. Look for body language messages as well as word messages?

___ 6. Steer clear of needing to have the last word?

___ 7. Make a conscious effort to consider and question the logic and credibility of what you hear?

___ 8. Ask for clarification when the words of the speaker have lost their meaning?

___ 9. Use active listening techniques, such as paraphrasing?

___ 10. Attempt to remember the significant points in the speaker's message?

50 is a perfect score. Less than 30 indicates that you could use more work in the area of listening skills.

9. Problem Solving

"Problems, Problems, Problems"

L ife brings problems with it. Each day we are faced with challenges that may cause individual stress or organizational disharmony. This stems in great part from the tone set by the group leadership and the current approach used to solve problems.

An important point to recognize is that problems will never be solved until such time as they are identified and dealt with openly. It is the responsibility of the group leader to set the climate for the group, to approach problems as challenges, and to make it OK to acknowledge that there is a problem. Until this is done the problem will not be solved, more likely it will perpetuate itself.

This chapter includes material on approaches to problem solving. None of the techniques is useful until it is actually put to use by a group. And, those assigned to tackle the problem(s) should have certain characteristics if results are to be expected.

They should have:

1. A commitment to the organization

2. A sense of significance in the group

3. A vested interest in finding a solution

4. An open, creative and cooperative nature

5. A logical, analytical mind

6. And a general sense of fairness

SIX STEP PROCESS

Problem solving is making a selection from a choice of alternatives. It should be thought of as a Process which includes six steps:

1. *Defining the problem:* Few problems are clearcut, and many times the symptoms are more apparent than the causes. These symptoms offer valuable *clues* to underlying problems, but not the real problem.

2. *Gathering facts and data:* Decision-making requires that you gather all the data that might have a bearing on the problem. For the most part, this will consist of facts, opinions and assumptions obtained from observations, records or other people. If essential information is not available, it is best to delay your decision until you acquire it.

3. *Organizing the information:* If you are working with many facts or considerable data, you'll have to sort out the important from the trivial, and organize the information so it can be compared and analyzed. As you study what's available, you should look for relationships among the various factors, such as costs, growth, schedules, advantages and disadvantages.

4. *Developing alternate solutions:* Develop as many good options as possible. Quality and quantity are equally important. Most problems have more than one solution. The important thing is to keep an open mind; let your imagination roam freely over the facts you've collected, and record possible solutions as they occur to you.

5. *Analyzing the alternatives and making a decision:* Now, compare the alternatives and determine the best solution. Test the alternatives against specific criteria, the risk involved, permanency of the remedy, timing, practicality, your objectives, etc. Eliminate the unacceptable options and focus on a few acceptable alternatives. Ultimately, you will arrive at the best decision.

6. *Evaluating the effectiveness of the chosen solution.* If necessary try another alternative. Be willing to work toward a true "win/win" solution. Periodic reassessment is perfectly appropriate ... circumstances change.

TECHNIQUES FOR PROBLEM SOLVING

1. Systematic or Traditional
a)   State or define the problem
b)   State rules that apply, if there are any
c)   Gather/state facts that bear on the problem
d)   Propose alternate solutions
e)   Evaluate those solutions
f)   Recommend and support suggested solution, **Action**
g)   Evaluate — repeat process if necessary

2. Brainstorming
(used most often in connection with the Systematic method in developing alternatives)
a)   Everyone involved presents ideas; these are recorded.
b)   No negative comments may be made.
c)   Ideas may be "piggy-backed". One person may enlarge on another's idea.
d)   On completion of feed-in phase, ideas are evaluated, possibly combined.
e)   Group selects the best idea based upon agreed criteria and puts it into action. **Action.**

3. Force Field Analysis
a)   Define the problem.
    Is it something you really care about?
    Are you personally involved?
    Is it possible to influence the situation?
b)   Describe it as it is now, and as you would like it to be. Restate it, indicating the direction of change.
c)   List forces that affect your situation.

Restraining Forces	**Driving Forces**
Forces that resist improvement	Forces which push toward improvement

d)   Review and underline 2 or 3 that seem most important right now and which you might be able to effect constructively.
e)   For each Restraining Force underlined, list possible action that might reduce the effect or eliminate it.

Restraining Force A-	**Restraining Force B-**
Possible Actions	**Possible Actions**

f)   Do the same for each driving force underlined. List action steps which would increase the effect of each Driving Force.

Driving Force A- Possible Actions	Driving Force B Possible Actions

The place to begin change is where stress and strain exist. Increased stress may be motivation for change. An attempt to increase a Driving Force may result only in parallel increase in opposing force.

g) Review action steps and underline those that seem promising.

h) List steps underlined. For each, list materials, people and resources available to help you carry out the action.

Action Steps	Resources

i) Plan a way of evaluating the effectiveness of the action program. Consider the consequence of your action *as well as any decision not to act.*

j) Implement your program. **Action.**

This method requires that you describe your situation as it is now, listing the positive (what will help you) and the negative (that working against you). Then, describe it as you would like it to be. Restate it indicating the direction of change, again noting "Restraining Forces" and "Driving Forces".

The next step is where constructive, creative thinking comes in. List possible action that might reduce the effect of Restraining Forces, or eliminate it. Then take the Driving Forces and consider how best you could increase the positive effect of each. Take charge. Become involved — don't simply become affected.

The really good thing about a Force Field Analysis is that the group leaves with each member going off to do a job, to help make something happen, or to intervene where trouble lurks.

4. Value Expectancy Grid

a) Define the problem.

b) Determine factors affecting the decision.

c) Assign them numerical values on a rating of 1-10, depending on their importance to you.

d) Determine possible alternate solutions.

e) Plot both on a simple graph.

f) Evaluate those chosen factors in each of the alternatives and assign them a numerical score.

g) Total the assigned scores and evaluate carefully the decision.

h) Implement the plan with the highest score. **Action.**

The Value Grid is preferred by those who are open to purely objective options.

VALUE EXPECTANCY GRID

	Factor #1	Factor #2	Factor #3	Factor #4	Factor #5
1-10					
Alt. #1					
Alt. #2					
Alt. #3					

5. PROBLEM ANALYSIS

a) Defining the problem

b) Establishing criteria — what you need to achieve, to maintain, and to avoid

c) List criteria in order of priority

d) Develop possible solutions

e) Review data pertinent to solution in terms of how it meets each criterion

f) Test for potential satisfaction of the problem

In problem solving, it is the job of the leader or facilitator to fully understand, without judgment, how the members of the group feel about each item discussed, and to create an atmosphere where all ideas are viewed as worthy of consideration and of potential value.

Analogies and metaphors are frequently helpful in generating productive ideas, as is Positive Imagery. Positive Imagery requires that you focus on what would be the best possible thing that could happen, then work backwards to figure out how to make it happen. It is important that the group be in agreement with the "image".

As you proceed to seek solutions to identified problems, remember that *each member cherishes his own individuality far more than any problem to be solved.* If his individuality becomes threatened, he will not only stop co-operating but become a problem to the task. It is for this reason that I recommend time be allotted for Team Building prior to any effort to do creative problem solving (see page 60). When all participants feel truly comfortable in the group, they will become less protective of *their ideas* and more willing to be objective as you progress through consideration of alternatives to selection of alternatives.

With Interaction Recording (see page 29) ideas are listed on a flip chart in front of the group and are then considered for their own value and removed from the individual generating the idea. This assures greater objectivity by members of the group.

CREATIVITY

A feeling of creative discontent can often lead to good solutions. The discontent is what will inspire us to seek a change (propose an alternative). The creative part is harder to work with because, like motivation, it comes from within.

Creativity must be *cultivated* within a group. To do this, a leader must:

1. Show he believes in the creative ability of the participants
2. Help break old habits and encourage new perspectives
3. Encourage innovation
4. Suspend premature judgment
5. Protect members from feeling foolish
6. Avoid criticism of individuals or their ideas
7. Discourage negative comments
8. Steer away from competitiveness within
9. Loosen rigid thinking
10. Bring confusion into focus

If you pre-plan for results, you will find that what looks like a problem will solve itself. Outlining the expected results puts you on a path toward success. It is also helpful to break routine. If routine approaches are coming in conflict with desired results, change the routine. For example, if fewer and fewer members seem to be attending your 9 a.m. meetings, try meeting at lunch, or in the evening or on Saturday. Find some time that produces a greater success ratio. (If in fact it is the *hour* that is the problem and not some other factor).

Logic, the ability to be quantitative, analytical and verbal and to conceptualize freely and think creatively are all useful traits in problem solving. This includes the ability to properly identify the problem, for if the problem is not properly identified, it will not be properly solved. This stems from the tendency to spend a minimum amount of effort on *problem definition* in order to get on with solving the problem.

Most problem solving is approached with fear and trepidation — if not a sense of crisis. Life is full of problems. Each day brings new problems. However, it is more productive to view each as a *challenge* and when talking about group or committee problems, we should try to be systematic in our approach.

Few people like problems, and as a result, there is a tendency to pick the first solutions that comes to mind. Consequently, this may lead to worse problems than before.

If you proceed to change your meeting time, having decided people aren't coming because of the hour, you may still have a low attendance. In fact, they may not be coming because they had expected great programs and you no longer provide them.

It would be a big help if Problem Solving were an exact science, but acknowledging that it is not is the first step in the solution. A second is to recognize that a major stumbling block to Problem Solution is the failure to first identify and agree upon the *criteria* for an acceptable solution. Once these are delineated, potential solutions can be weighed objectively.

- What do you want to achieve?
- What must you preserve?
- What do you seek to avoid?
- Which has more priority?

And, a third step is in reminding all concerned that their solution will be only as good as the information considered. Analytical minds will *not* create practical and productive solutions if their discussions are based on inaccurate or inadequate information.

FOUR LEVELS OF INFORMATION

Be conscious of the kind of information you're considering. Your solutions are only as good as the information on which they are based. There are four levels of information which you may consider when gathering data; these include:

A. FACT = That which has actual existence

B. INFERENCE = A logical conclusion based on fact

C. SPECULATION = A theory based on conjecture rather than fact

D. OPINION = A belief stronger than an impression

The material which is identified as OPINION is generally too subjective to be useful in Problem Solving. Your aim should be to gather all the FACTS, pertinent and available, and to make your decisions based on that information.

To make a wise decision:

- Know where you are going (objective)
- Know what has to be accomplished
- Know the alternate ways and means to get from here to there, and weigh these

Problem Solving is often tackled from a general brainstorming approach, with no focus. The problem as stated may be too big and beyond reach. To be realistic about it, divide a problem into manageable components.

A useful technique to help focus is to ask "why", and to keep asking "why" until you finally arrive at your real concern. "How can we build a better mouse trap?" is a fine problem, but if you ask "why", you discover you really mean "What is the best way to catch mice?", or even "How can we rid our homes of mice?", or "How can we keep our homes free of mice?" Do you see that each Problem Statement opens up a different focus, and thus a different solution?

Before you seek to solve your problem be quite sure you have truly identified the problem and not merely a *symptom* of the problem, and when you have, state it as a question.

The Problem Analysis Chart I have included on page 140 is designed to keep you focused on the real nature of your problem and to communicate with others your perception of the situation. By filling this out with a small group assigned to developing a proposed solution, you can chart your information in a useful manner, one that allows you to test each of your criteria against the possible solutions.

However, for everyone to "buy into" the chosen solution, those affected must be given the opportunity to be *heard*. Everyone is coming from a different set of priorities and experiences, and their willingness to help the solution work will depend on their investment in the selection of that solution. "Bottoms up is the bottom line." Listen to the ideas and feelings of those affected by the solution.

In creative problem solving, it is essential that we avoid thinking in absolutes and consider ideas on a spectrum from really good to very bad.

REALLY GOOD————————————————**VERY BAD**

Each consideration can then be placed, with consensus of the group, somewhere on the spectrum.

Synergism is also a great term to keep in mind when approaching a problem: "Mutually reinforcing action of separate agents or ideas which together produce an effect greater than that of all the components acting separately." I can think of some solutions. You can think of some solutions. But together, by sharing our ideas, we will create more than the total of your ideas and my ideas. We can build on all the ideas for still other, better ideas.

Any of the above approaches can be successful. The situation will decide which is best. In any case a conscious approach, rather than a haphazard, crisis approach, is what will assure the selection of a successful solution.

The best way to produce change is to come up with an alternative that everyone prefers to whatever is happening now. To encourage positive, creative thinking within your group, you might begin by asking that they come to you with solutions rather than problems. This gives them the feeling you trust them to identify their problems and have faith in their ability to generate potential solutions. Always respect the individuals more than the structure. *Listen.* And remember that for someone to win, (by having his solution selected) someone else need not lose, because the productive solution will benefit everyone.

As a leader or chairman you needn't feel it is your responsibility to make all judgments, solve all problems and hand out all edicts, but rather to help your co-workers spot problems and work together to devise alternatives and seek solutions. In Problem Solving *cooperation* should be encouraged and *competition* discouraged.

It is my contention that the chairman or leader who brings an attitude of cheerfulness, understanding and cooperation to each situation, will find his co-workers reflecting these in return.

A good chairman will seek to develop a sense of confident respect for himself and others, and an appreciation of individuals and their differences. If we don't respect our committee workers, we can hardly expect them to demonstrate respect for us or our project. We need to appreciate the worth of others.

It is difficult to see a problem from the point of view of others; however, it is an essential consideration in conceptualizing, and it leads to a better solution because it takes into consideration more interests representing other individuals. The solution will be acted upon more readily if it represents the expressed feelings of all affected.

In Problem Solving between two people, the ability to see the problem from the other's point of view is the key. Gain a feeling for the viewpoint of the other in order to come to an acceptable solution. Always ask yourself how the other might be viewing the issue, and from what bias, from what value base. If in doubt — ASK!

BLOCKS TO PROBLEM SOLVING

Adapted from material by James L. Adams in Conceptual Blockbusting, a Guide to Better Ideas, with permission of the author and the publisher, W.W. Norton & Co., Inc., N.Y., N.Y. Copyright © 1974, 1976, 1979 by James L. Adams

Perceptual Blocks

- *Difficulty in isolating the problem:* Is the meeting attendance problem one of when it is held?, or maybe what is offered?, or where it is held, or even who is handling it? Weigh ALL of the possibilities.

- *Tendency to limit the problem area too closely:* Have you failed to consider peripheral aspects of the situation — things which at first glance may not appear to be related to the problem?

- *Inability to see the problem from various points of view:* Have you taken the time to consider how each of the others involved might view the situation?

- *Seeing what you expect to see:* (Stereotyping) Have you tried altering your focus or changing your point of view? Try painting a portrait from a photo turned upside down. You will see what is there — not what you expect to be there.

- *Saturation:* Many extremely familiar things are not recorded in our memories in ways that allow easy recall. Can you identify the letters that go with the numbers on your phone. . .without looking?

- *Failure to utilize all sensory input:* Our senses are interconnected — taste becomes inhibited when smell is suppressed, and in reverse — sight is augmented by supplementary sound.

We also suffer from Cultural, Environmental and Emotional Blocks.

Cultural Blocks

Cultural blocks are those which bring judgment into play. This judgment is generally confining and responsible for squelching creativity. Among the most common cultural blocks are the ideas that:

1. Logic, reason, practicality, utility are GOOD; pleasure, feelings, qualitative judgments are BAD.

2. Fantasy and reflection are a waste of time.

3. Playfulness is childish.

4. Problem Solving is serious business; humor has no place in it.

5. Tradition is preferable to change.

6. Any problem can be solved by scientific thinking and lots of money.

7. Taboos.

Unless we are aware of these we may be hindered in our efforts to solve our problems. There is considerable evidence that suggests fantasy, reflection and mental playfulness are *essential* to creative thinking and productive conceptualization. Unfortunately, these properties are frequently "socialized" out of people after childhood. Unless people are lucky enough to work with others who encourage creativity and reward them for innovative ideas, they are apt to be stifled and creative problem solving is less likely to take place.

Environmental Blocks

1. Autocratic leaders who value only their own ideas and fail to reward others.

2. A lack of cooperation and trust among co-workers.

3. Lack of support that would bring ideas to action.

4. Distractions such as telephones and other easy intrusions.

Effective conceptualization requires that a combination of previously unrelated structures be seen a new way, incorporating logic and reason with intuition and feeling.

Motivation is essential in creativity. Unless those involved truly want to solve the problem and see that they will be affected by the effort in a positive way, they will probably bring little enthusiasm to the task. Thus it is essential that those ultimately challenged to work out a possible solution, based on input from everyone affected, be those in your group who bring the greatest interest and motivation to the task. Unless a member is truly convinced that a change is needed, he is not likely to hypothesize ways to bring about a change.

I can't stress enough the importance of support. Non-supportive responses, especially from chairmen or other authority figures, are very harmful to creative problem solving. Most people are at least somewhat unsure of the quality of their own ideas and therefore require a supportive environment in which to work.

An atmosphere of honesty, trust and support is absolutely necessary if people are going to be encouraged to be creative in conceptualizing solutions. A friendly, non-competitive, interactive situation helps to encourage people to generate new ideas and to have the courage to express them. For these reasons a chairman must praise and reward all the participants for their efforts.

As if Environmental, Perceptual and Cultural Blocks were not enough to stand in our way of Problem Solving, we also face **Emotional Blocks**, of which a chairman must be aware.

Emotional Blocks

- Fear of failure
- Desire for order and security (inability to tolerate ambiguity)
- Preference for judging ideas, rather than generating them
- Lack of challenge (no motivation)
- Inability to relax and incubate ideas
- Lack of access to areas of imagination
- Excessive zeal; eagerness to succeed quickly
- Inability to distinguish reality from fantasy
- Lack of imaginative control
- Need at all times to feel we are right

Most of us have been rewarded when we produced right answers, and punished when we made mistakes. When we failed, we were made to feel we had let others down. Somehow we must begin to provide a non-judgmental environment (— so all ideas are given consideration), and allowed to generate options different from the norm.

Fear of making mistakes is rooted in insecurity and such insecurities are responsible for the inability to tolerate ambiguity. Finding the solution to a complex problem can be a messy process, and in a sense, problem solving is bringing order out of chaos. The ability to tolerate some chaos seems to be necessary to creative thinking and productive problem solving.

Compulsive people who must always have everything in its place seem to be impaired in their ability to work with certain types of problems, if this trait is carried over to a person's mental process. The process of bringing widely disparate thoughts together cannot take place in a mind which will not allow incompatable thoughts to exist together long enough to combine.

We are all affected to a greater or lesser extent by each of the blocks cited above — EMOTIONAL, ENVIRONMENTAL, PERCEPTUAL and CULTURAL. Be aware of these and deal with the effects. If you recognize that you have on your committee or within your group people who are more objective than others and less affected by these typical blocks, they are probably your best resources for creative problem solving.

In addition, if you foresee annual or perpetual problem solving sessions, perhaps it is time to provide training in the skills needed to effectively handle this, as well as increase awareness of typical blocks to problem solving. We can't be expected to change our behavior or our approaches if we are unaware of alternate ways, or if we are not conscious of the failings in our current styles.

Creativity requires the manipulation and recombination of experience. The creative person needs the opportunity to fantasize freely and vividly. One of the most important capabilities in a creative person is a questioning attitude. Unfortunately, many adults resist asking questions because it is an admission of ignorance. Again, constructive discontent is productive. (Dumb questions are easier to handle than dumb mistakes!)

You have nothing to lose and a great deal to gain by questioning. When you begin to question things, you can also look at situations from new angles. Try adapting, modifying, magnifying, minifying, combining, rearranging and reversing.

Exercise your own mind. Begin to apply some of these strategies. Stretch your mind to begin to hold many ideas at one time — in some confusion — and allow these to germinate and to interplay with all others. This will help you to become better at Problem Solving.

CHECK LIST FOR NEW IDEAS

Below is a check list which can be applied to the thinking process to be sure that you have not been trapped by one of the blocks. It is great for *innovation* rather than *evaluation*. The material below is adapted from *APPLIED IMAGINATION* by Alex Osborn with the permission of Charles Scribner's Sons, Copyright © 1953, 1957, 1963 by Charles Scribner's Sons; copyright renewed 1981 by Russell Osborn.

Modify: New twist? Change meaning, color, motion, sound, odor, form, shape? Other changes?

Magnify: What to add? More time? Greater frequency? Stronger? Higher? Longer? Thicker? Extra value? Plus ingredient? Duplicate? Multiply? Exaggerate?

Minify: What to subtract? Smaller? Condense? Miniature? Lower? Shorter? Lighter? Omit? Streamline? Split up? Understate?

Adapt: What else is like this? What other ideas does this suggest? Does past offer a parallel? What could I copy? Whom could I emulate?

Reverse: Transpose positive and negative? How about opposites? Turn it backwards? Turn it upside down? Reverse roles? Change shoes? Turn tables? Turn other cheek?

Put to other uses: New ways to use as is? Other uses if modified?

Rearrange: Interchange components? Other pattern? Other layout? Other sequence? Change pace? Change schedule? Transpose cause and effect?

Substitute: Who else instead? What else instead? Other material? Other ingredient, other process? Other place? Other approach? Other power? Other tone of voice?

Combine: How about a blend, an alloy, an assortment, an ensemble? Combine units? Combine purposes? Combine ideas? Combine appeals?

These ideas need not apply simply to products in the business world, but can be used to consider projects and fund raisers which have always been profitable but perhaps need a new angle.

PROBLEM SOLVING PROBLEMS

adapted from *Problem Solving & Group Interaction*
by Bobby R. Patton and Kim Giffin (used with permission)

The following is a list of reasons why your group may be limited in its ability to solve a particular problem or problems. By referring to this list you may be able to identify a specific area that needs attention. Remember that a "process" is only as effective as the people who are using it.

I.   Personal and Interpersonal Attitudes and Behavior
    A. Individual needs for identity, recognition and security
    B. Severely competitive behavior
    C. Need to dominate others
    D. Overly defensive behavior
    E. Inaccurate interpersonal perceptions (one member may think another is threatening)
    F. Lack of attraction by the group for some members
    G. Unreasonable conformity to group pressures
    H. Poor communication

II. Identification of the problem to task
    A. Lack of mutual concern or lack of *any* concern
    B. Lack of cohesiveness in the group regarding the problem
    C. Inability to overcome confusion

III. Definition of the Problem
    A. Failure to compare what is, with what is desired
    B. Inability to agree on the scope of the problem
    C. Inability to agree on the severity of the problem
    D. Lack of factual information (too much reliance on unverified opinions and guesses)

IV. Generation and Selection of Solutions
    A. Lack of identification of possible solutions (inexperience in the area or lack of creative thinking)

      B. Poor identification of criteria for evaluating solutions

      C. Inability to agree on a group decision

V. Implementation of Group Decision

      A. Inability to sort and allocate resources

      B. Inability to agree upon individual members' responsibilities

      C. Inability to persuade others to give support, approval, aid

VI. Role Functions

      A. Inability to agree on who is to perform leadership functions

      B. Poor match between member's personality and role requirements

VII. Group Characteristics

      A. Group is too large or too small

      B. Poor cohesiveness

      C. Lack of status or prestige of the group

      D. Unacceptable group norms (such as tardiness, absenteeism, discourtesy)

      E. On-going power struggle

      F. Lack of individual commitment

      G. General apathy

VIII. Conflict Within the Group

      A. Inability to discriminate between honest disagreement and interpersonal dislike

      B. Inability to be comfortable with honest, reasonable disagreement

IX. Selection of Appropriate Discussion Modes

      A. Inability to choose alternate formats for group thinking (such as brainstorming, leaderless discussion, sub-groupings, committees)

      B. Inability to structure discussions

      C. Too much leader dominance of discussion

One of the wonderfully naive things about most of us is our belief that simply by forming a committee or establishing a Task Force *any* problem can be solved. It just isn't so. Too often we must actually settle for the best option available. . .and it may not truly be a solution. All problems do not have solutions, per se. However, this is not to say we should stop looking or that we should resign ourselves to troubles which spring eternal. Just identifying the existence of a problem puts us closer to a solution than before it was openly acknowledged.

The following two forms are for use in sessions with groups interested in accurately identifying their problems, criteria for an acceptable solution, and in generating possible solutions.

PROBLEM ANALYSIS CHART
(For Decision Making)

		4. Solutions — Identify ways we could meet our criteria			
		A.	**B.**	**C.**	**D.**
1.	**Definition of Problem**				
2.	**CRITERIA** — What we need to... ACHIEVE				
	PRESERVE				
	AVOID				
	...by whatever we decide to do				
3.	**PRIORITIES:** List the relative importance of the criteria.				

5. **DATA:** What we know about each solution as to how it meets each of our criteria

6. **TEST:** Take each of the criteria one at a time and consider the relative degree of satisfaction provided by each solution. Which will be the best overall?

Problem-Solving Guide

Purpose: To find a no-lose solution to conflict.

Directions: Use this worksheet to guide and record your feelings as well as those of others affected by the decision.

Step 1. Identify Needs:

Yours	Others'

Step 2. Brainstorm Solutions: Step 3. Evaluate Solutions (✔):

Solutions	Acceptable	Not Acceptable
	☐ ☐ ☐ ☐ ☐ ☐ ☐ ☐ ☐ ☐ ☐	☐ ☐ ☐ ☐ ☐ ☐ ☐ ☐ ☐ ☐ ☐

Step 4. Choose Solution: Step 5. Plan of Action: Step 6. Assessment of Results:

Who?

What?

When?

Used with permission of copyright holder, Effectiveness Training, Inc., 531 Stevens Avenue, Solana Beach, CA.

10. Time Management

"It's About Time"

T ime management is really much easier to discuss in a workshop than a handbook. This is because what we value, what priorities we hold and how we use our time will greatly affect our *view* of time.

There are national seminar leaders who promote the idea of "working smarter" to assure more productive use of our time, and helping others to do the same. To me, this really means simply being aware of what you are doing with your time. It will slip away if you don't plan for the careful use of the hours you do have.

HOW TO MANAGE YOUR TIME

If you don't manage your time, it will be managed for you. It will be scheduled and stolen by others who need you, and the hours for all those things you wished you had accomplished will have evaporated. Set goals for yourself and share these with others.

The real key to success here is in doing some planning. A form of objective setting — what do you want to accomplish? By when? If you don't say it, or state it, it is not likely to ever happen. Make a commitment to goals.

The list makers of the world are on the right track because they at least have set out to do something. They may not have concluded that some things are more important than others, but they know what they would like to do, and that is a start.

One of the first things to remember when planning your time or simply wondering, "Where does my time go?", *is that our value system greatly affects the way we use our time.*

If you value harmony you may spend a considerable part of your day acting as an arbitrator, in an attempt to keep peace. If you value praise, you may put your greatest energies into those things which will be noticed by others. If you value neatness, a considerable portion of your day may be spent in housekeeping tasks.

Because we all value different things, it is important to recognize and acknowledge these differences, especially in those with whom we live and work. It is also important to communicate these feelings with them — if you want their cooperation in maintaining a certain standard. We can't presume that others feel as we do, or that they even know how we feel.

Equally important is the fact that some things are not valued at all. And when these come in conflict with things you hold as important, problems can certainly be expected. Two come quickly to mind — time and money.

As we work in the community with others, we soon find that there are some who 1) would rather invest their money than give of their time, 2) would rather give of their time than invest any money, 3) do not place too much consideration on the money involved, and this can mean *your* money for such things as sitters or material goods, 4) seem to have considerable time to waste — those who don't seem to pre-plan events and as a result, everyone's time is unwisely spent.

VALUE OF TIME

If you begin to value time, you'll invest it wisely. In my workshops we always have the participants think for a minute about the idea that their time is worth money. What if you were given $1,440 every day — and told if you didn't spend it that day, you would have to return it? Every day you would be given another $1,440. How would you spend it? This is how many minutes you will find in each day and if you haven't invested them — you have lost them. You can't come back tomorrow and say, "You know the 2 hours that slipped away after I cleaned up the breakfast dishes? I need them today."

TIME INVESTMENT

Time invested in the *process* of living is as important as the tangible, measurable things. Good relationships don't just happen, they take time, and pay great rewards. Don't diminish the value of things you can't measure. To sit on the porch and watch the sun go down may seem unproductive to some — but if it leaves you rejuvenated and ready to give your all to a project, then it is time well spent. If it brings you closer to those near to you, or helps you to understand someone you work with, it's time well spent. We all value different things, and because of this, we will invest our time differently.

TIME PRIORITIES

If you are aggravated with yourself for wasting time, perhaps you have never taken the time to set down specifically what you want to accomplish. Make lists. Be reasonable. You'll only assure disappointment if your list is unrealistic. Keeping a calendar for commitments can help you to balance your time.

Once you know what you want to do, you can then consider how you want to go about accomplishing these things. A check list, in order, can save your back-tracking. It can also be helpful in deciding on priorities.

"What is the best use of my time RIGHT NOW?", is a question you should ask yourself often. By remaining flexible, you can shift from one project to another, depending on the interferences which complicate your day. Carrying something with you to do if you must wait (under a dryer, in a doctor's office, waiting for an appointment, etc.) can give you a feeling of accomplishment and reduce stress. Answer neglected letters, catch up on leisure reading. Make a list of "Things To Do."

BLOCKS OF TIME

One real key to accomplishing a great deal is the use of small blocks of time. Some people seem to say, "There really isn't time to start anything." It is better to look at situations as *found time*. Be aware of the many things you face that can be done a little at a time, and keep these things handy.

DELEGATING

The next major time saver is delegating. To save time acknowledge that there is no way you can do everything, and do the things you want to do most. Delegate some tasks to people around you. It builds responsibility and encourages consideration.

Of course, it is time lost if the individual assigned is unable or fails to accomplish the assigned task, to your satisfaction. So we have a few rules to remember when delegating:

- CHOOSE people capable of handling the job.
- CLARIFY your expectations; they should be clearly understood.
- BELIEVE in the individual's ability to carry out the task.
- COMMIT the individual to the promise of following through.
- SET DEADLINES and stick to them.
- ALLOW LATITUDE and encourage initiative.
- FOLLOW UP; keep on top of the assignment.
- DON'T DO IT for them.
- REWARD the individual in keeping with the results produced.

TIME WASTERS

Obviously, one of the primary reasons we don't accomplish all we would like to is that we allow time wasters to steal our precious hours and minutes.

Procrastination — is one notorious time waster. By setting a time limit, a deadline for yourself, with specific goals, you will be less likely to procrastinate. You might also reward yourself when you have finished a task — or try doing the worst jobs first.

Misunderstandings. When receiving or giving assignments, make a supreme effort to assure yourself that everyone involved fully understands. If things aren't done right the first time, when will you have time to do them over? (see Communication chapter)

Interruptions. If you need to work in isolation, go to the neighborhood library. If you have things to do at home, but the telephone persists in ringing ... turn it off! A note on the door can politely discourage coffee callers. Schedule your activities so that you will be alone when quiet is needed, and when you can deal with interruptions, do things that aren't affected by having others around.

Lack of Preparation. Plan before meeting with others; know what points you need to cover and what answers you want — and expect the same of them. Let them know you are busy and it is important to you that they give things some advance thought. Mentally walk yourself through events to establish what needs you'll face with the actual situation.

Perfection — reduces your productivity rate. Consider frankly just how important perfection is to each task facing you. Extreme perfection is an unrealistic use of time. This is not to suggest that you compromise your standards — just be realistic.

Clutter. If you can't find it, you lose considerable time searching. "A place for everything and everything in its place" — is ideal, including the waste basket! (Must you save everything?) Also, consider setting up a personal file box with folders for such things as Bank, Car, Utilities, House, Taxes, School, Club.

Lack of Energy — unless you invest some time in your own good health — eating right, exercising, getting enough sleep — then you will have fewer hours to count on.

Decisions. If too many basic decisions require your attention, you all lose time. Help develop in others the ability to make decisions at the lowest level possible, and to bring you solutions, not problems. Ask how *they* would solve the problem.

There are really no shortcuts, and time management doesn't happen without effort. You must be aware of how much time you have and how you want to use it, and you must invest a little time in planning ahead to save considerable time.

HELPFUL HINTS FOR TIME MANAGEMENT

To find those extra hours needed, to fulfill yourself as a volunteer in a community which reminds you that you're needed, you're appreciated, you're special, you may have to shift your priorities a little. Consider the following:

- Have something constructive to do with small blocks of time.

- Keep "busy work" activities near the phone (polish, handiwork, mending, etc.)

- Anticipate — when shopping. Load up (potential gifts, especially childrens', future birthday cards, frequently used items such as soap and toothpaste) and plan your trips to town in a logical order.

- Invest in a 25 ft. telephone cord that will provide you with mobility while on the phone (or better yet a cordless phone!)

- When bogged down — move on; go to something else.
- Consider doing two things at once — change beds while doing a load of laundry.
- Have people bring you potential solutions rather than problems.
- Set specific, realistic objectives to be accomplished each day.
- Keep your long-range goals in mind while doing your smallest task.
- *Clarify*, don't waste time because of misunderstood instructions.
- Make a realistic estimate of your time available; don't set yourself up for failure.
- Set priorities and plan for the best time to accomplish the most important tasks.
- Learn to say "no", and don't feel guilty.
- Select the best time of day for the type of work required.
- Build on success and don't waste time regretting failures.
- Think positively about the success of your goal, whatever it is.
- Help those around you to develop a sense of independence and faith in themselves.
- Make decisions at the lowest level possible, and train others to make decisions without you.
- Remember that time spent organizing and planning pays off in time saved later.
- Do it now!
- Approach household chores as a collection of small tasks rather than one overwelming project.
- Make specific lists of things to do today — check them off.
- Don't allow others to steal your time; explain, if you're busy, and get on with your projects.
- Learn who can handle responsibility, and delegate often.
- Continually ask yourself, "Am I making the best use of my time *right now?*".

PERSONAL TIME LOG

DATE:	VOLUNTEER RELATED						PERSONAL					KEEP HANDY FOR RECORDING NOTES, COMMENTS ON OPPORTUNITIES FOR IMPROVEMENT
GOALS: 1. 2. 3. 4. 5. 6.	ROUTINE WORK	COMMUNICATION	TELEPHONE	PLANNING	ACTION & DECISIONS	OUTSIDE ACTIVITIES	PHYSICAL HEALTH	FAMILY	LEISURE ACTIVITIES	PERSONAL GROWTH	OTHER	
6:00 a.m. 6:30												
7:00 7:30												
8:00 8:30												
9:00 9:30												
10:00 10:30												
11:00 11:30												
12:00 p.m. 12:30												
1:00 1:30												
2:00 2:30												
3:00 3:30												
4:00 4:30												
5:00 5:30												
6:00 p.m. 6:30												
7:00 7:30												
8:00 8:30												
9:00 9:30												
10:00 10:30												
11:00												
TOTAL HOURS												

Record for a week the amount of time spent in each area. Make comments to yourself about how you might improve the situation.

11. Management by Objectives

"In the Beginning ..."

"Pick battles big enough to matter, but small enough to win."

Management by Objectives is a yardstick by which to measure the results of projects or programs. It is a credible method for determining how well organizations and agencies have achieved their mission. It is also a systematic way to plan that anticipates positive results.

MBO is a system which helps groups to clarify their purpose and goals. It allows members to identify achievable objectives that demonstrate their effectiveness, and measures the results.

Accountability is essential for incorporated non-profit agencies in order to maintain a tax-exempt status. And it is also necessary if organizations are to convince donors (individual, corporate and foundation) that theirs is a worthy cause. There is considerable competition for dollars and donors, and in each case the demand will be made to, "Show me why I should donate to your agency, over ABC's?"

Because agencies are 'nonprofit' there lies a misconception that there is no real need for money or manpower management, or accountability. But there is. To survive, not-for-profit organizations must become every bit as effective and accountable as commercial businesses.

Management by objectives is a system businessmen have perfected. It is an equally useful tool for the volunteer. In this chapter I have tried to simplify an explanation of just how this can be adapted by the volunteer and to provide an outline with which to work.

Nonprofit organizations, like any organization, have a mission or purpose, and objectives to achieve. These objectives relate to delivering the highest quality service possible with a realistic expenditure of time, energy and money. Managers and Boards of non-profit agencies have a responsibility to utilize, in a prudent manner, any available assets, and to be accountable for results.

Initiating a management approach based on objective setting may not be easy. It requires considerable pre-planning. However, failure to invest this time and to develop a clear cut set of objectives will invite potential problems and may perpetuate crisis management.

INITIAL CONSIDERATIONS

To set up an MBO (Management By Objectives) approach in your organization begin by setting a specific time for your executive committee (or a Task Force) to consider:

1. What is our mission or purpose?
2. What Key Result Areas do we want to address?
3. What realistic goals can we establish?
4. What reasonable, measurable objectives could we propose to the Board? (Remember, the plan, approach, or strategy should be developed by those responsible for the outcome).
5. What time frames could be attached to each objective?
6. To whom could we assign the authority for making this happen?
7. How can we periodically measure our progress in achieving these objectives?
8. Who will be responsible for evaluating the success in meeting this objective? By when?

KEY RESULT AREAS

The first consideration, before setting goals or establishing objectives, is that of identifying "Key Results Areas".* Dale McConkey goes into depth about this in his book *How to Manage by Results.*

As with the process of actually establishing objectives, this takes time. But it will save time and frustration in the long run. Set a meeting with your planning committee and devote it to identifying "Key Results Areas". These are areas of consideration in which it is absolutely essential that a high level of performance be assured; they are matters of highest priority. The purpose is to help the chairman to direct his limited resources (i.e. money, manpower, materials, time and authority) in a manner where the greatest return is assured, to identify what is truly important *before* writing objectives.

It is essential to think in positive terms. We want *results*.

> Results —not procedures
> Results —not the process
> Results —not the activities
> What   —not how
> Ends   —not means
> Output —not input

With "Key Result" considerations the focus is on *ultimate accomplishments*. When ideas are listed they usually fall into one or more of four general categories: 1) quantity, 2) quality, 3) cost, and 4) timeliness.

One word of caution, avoid considering any *measurement*. This is premature at this stage. As with problem solving, when it is advised that you suspend judgment during your first phase, measurements should be specified in your objectives. At this stage you are interested in identifying subject matter. Your concern needs to be in selecting the *areas* where the highest level of performance is essential.

-S.W.O.T.-
SITUATIONAL ANALYSIS

*Adapted by permission of the publisher from McConkey, Dale D., HOW TO MANAGE BY RESULTS, 3rd ed. (New York AMACOM, a division of American Management Associations, 1977), pp. 64-74.

After you have identified your Key Result Areas, analyze your capability of actually achieving a high level of performance. For this we have S.W.O.T.

We want to know what advantages we'll enjoy during this project. These are STRENGTHS and OPPORTUNITIES. Equally important is anticipation of disadvantages facing us, WEAKNESSES and THREATS. Each of your Key Results Areas should be analyzed for Strengths, Weaknesses, Opportunities and Threats. The first two are concerned with the present, and the second are geared toward the future.

Strengths — are those advantages operating in a favorable manner on which you should capitalize.

Weaknesses — are disadvantages which will impede performance and must be hurdled.

Opportunities — are future advantages which should be used to your best ability.

Threats — are future happenings or changes that may have a significant impact on your success. An attempt should be made to minimize these.

A careful SWOT analysis should help identify subject matter for your objectives and provide a guide as to the level of achievement you can realistically expect. It can also help you to set priorities.

An example of a "S.W.O.T. Analysis" for a hypothetical group might be:

KEY RESULT AREA	— A full staff of volunteers for all identified opportunities
Strengths	— Excellent facility
	— Convenient location
Weaknesses	— No public transportation
	— Greatest need: late night volunteers
Opportunities	— A growing community — Nearby college with internship needs
Threats	— Other local social service agencies in the same building draw from the same volunteer pool
	— More and more volunteers are getting paid jobs

Behavioral scientists have noted that man is very capable of self direction and control in reaching objectives ... *if* they are things to which he is committed. Individuals are willing to accept and even seek responsibility under encouraging conditions. Establishing an accepting and trusting environment in which ideas and solutions can flourish is one of the challenges of volunteer leadership.

It would be worth the effort to contact a local resource person to either provide a training workshop in MBO in advance of this session, or to facilitate an objective setting session with you. Organizations currently using MBO may have volunteers willing to work with you. Such groups as the Junior League, the United Way, the Red Cross and the Y might be considered. Local colleges or universities may have someone on staff willing to help you, as might a delegate from the Retired Senior Executives' pool or Small Business Administration. There are also nationally qualified trainers (such as your author) who deal exclusively with non-profit organizations.

If this all sounds overwhelmingly confusing, it is only because it may be new to you. As with Interaction Recording, try it — you'll like it, I promise. ANY pre-planning you can do pays off in the long run. It may seem like time you can't find — but if you fail to invest it in the beginning, you'll pay for it later.

OBJECTIVE SETTING

One of the major pitfalls of most volunteer Boards is their failure to spell out clearly 1) what they want to accomplish, 2) by what date, and 3) how they can measure this.

Frequently the charge is — "Let's have a carnival! We've done it every year. Who can we get to do it this year?" With turnover what it is, you'll probably discover that last year's coordinator has moved to Podunk and taken all his expertise with him . . . in his head.

Or . . . maybe, if you're luckier than many, he turned in a one-page report that listed all of those who helped, and maybe a little about how many booths there were and the kind of prizes they gave out. Oh, and the fact that they made $312 for the PTA treasury.

But wouldn't it have been helpful to know if it took all year, burned out a dozen volunteers, cost $750 to produce, was too hot in the middle of the basketball courts at noon in May, and that the kids never had a chance to help?

Besides a well thought-out proposal in advance of the "how to's", (including the allocation of basic resources: money, manpower, materials, time and authority) you'll never know whether it's time well spent if you don't set clear objectives before you start. Do you want to make money? How much money? Use volunteers? How many? Is having fun important? Involving the students?

Make sure you've stated your objectives so well that you could hand them to a totally uninvolved person and they would be absolutely clear, with no surprises or presumed areas of understanding. *Nothing* goes without saying. Spell out your expectations in the beginning.

This is also important in committee or Board work of any kind. To assure yourself of an interested, enthusiastic group, spell out clearly the requirements of each position and your expectations as a chairman concerning meetings, attendance, research, participation, involvement. By the same token, the group member has every right to know what he can expect from you in terms of clarification, support, standing behind him, etc.

The challenge to every volunteer leader is to gain skill in dealing effectively with tasks, learning to be a positive goal oriented manager, while being sensitive to the people who make things happen. In other words, to become an Executive! A volunteer executive is no different than a business executive. He has a responsibility to his agency or organization as well as to the people who staff it, volunteer and paid.

THE MANAGEMENT PROCESS

Management vs. Leadership

There is a distinct difference between Management and Leadership, although the words are often used synonomously. Leadership deals with motivating people to achieve some goal. It is concerned with only one commodity — people, their needs and emotions. Management deals with organizing resources in a specific, intelligent manner to achieve goals effectively. The primary emphasis is on getting results. A comparison of management versus leadership will show the difference.

Management	Leadership
essentially intellectual	essentially emotional
appointive office with power from above	elective with power from the people
stable	temporary — leadership rotates
analytical/problem solving	function of empathy
focuses on results	focuses on people
a science, concerned with task	an art, creative/innovative
rewarded by achievement & results	rewarded by personal relationships

Management is a problem solving system based in logic. Our effectiveness as managers is predicated on our willingness to discipline ourselves to adhere to the system, processes and controls of the science. Some lucky souls are *Executives* and fully qualified and skilled at leading as well as managing.

An Executive

Goal oriented	Decides
Thoughtful	Uses staff work
Results oriented	Directs
Effective	Mediates
Long-term planner	Represents organization
Mission oriented	Sees whole
Attracts talent	Operates in internal
Works in future	& external politics
Manages resources	Synthesizes
Studies environment	Concept oriented

AN ANALYTICAL SYSTEM

The management process is nothing more than an analytical system of organizing resources to get results, and it can be learned through study and discipline. It takes a lot of practice to do it well, but the rewards are enormous. Its chief advantage is that it forces you to verbalize exactly what it is you want to do *before* you jump into planning and actually doing the job.

Use of the Management Process:

- Assures that programs and projects will be well managed and plans continued, despite turnover in personnel
- Increases motivation
    a. members have advance knowledge of what is expected
    b. members are involved in overall planning and determination of standards used in evaluating performance
    c. emphasis is on results rather than methods employed in achieving them — encourages innovation
    d. achievements are easily measured
- Requires planning; minimizes crisis management
- Provides clear, mutual understanding on matters of procedure
- Gives members a sense of direction and security; knowledge of where they are, where they are going, and why
- Operates with a minimum of lost or wasted effort or resources
- Builds in future planning, due to cyclical nature
- Is adaptable to personal, voluntary or business life

OBJECTIVES

The most difficult job in management is translating an organization's *goals*, its general statements of intent, into defined and specific *objectives* before initiating any planning or tackling any job. Such objectives must direct activity and contain specific figures and standards that are meaningful to the people whose progress and results are to be measured. A committee has a clearly defined and communicated objective when every member can answer:

1. What will be different or achieved upon completion?
2. What is the time limit?
3. How will the difference be measured?

Where are objectives set? The Board of Directors should set the organization's Board objectives and each committee person can work out objectives and plans to meet these Board objectives. Organizational objectives are more complex to set than personal ones, because organizations by nature encompass the aspirations and efforts of many. Some objectives are quite properly in the domain of one committee, some the whole organization.

Many committee objectives are limiting ones, offering strategies (how something will be accomplished) as part of the objective. Board objectives should never include any strategy in the statement of what will be different. Many times objectives are not fulfilled in one year, and in some cases different people will be carrying them out, as tends to happen with a rotating Board. However, this is the beauty of the management process; it is designed for future planning, each year building on the previous one.

It is important that objectives be realistic. If they are not realistically attainable, they will only produce frustration. If, on the other hand, they are too easily reached, then there is no challenge and they will not move the organization forward.

Specifying objectives at the outset ensures that the entire committee or Board knows what it is trying to do, and enables decisions, policies and priorities to be made in the light of what it is the group is trying to accomplish.

PLAN OF ACTION

Once you have a clear objective, with a time frame and measurement, planning involves walking through the experience *backward.* You know what you want to have happen at the other end. So *how* are you going to make it happen? Planning a blueprint is necessary to achieve your objectives. Inherent in any good plan are four basic considerations:

1. Decide what overall strategy the group will use to accomplish the task.

2. Allocate the various resources as needed.

3. Establish a monitoring system to warn of impending failure.

4. Formulate alternate plans for use when monitoring system indicates performance is not meeting expectation.

Strategy is nothing more than a statement as to *how* the plan will be achieved. Several strategies may fit the objective, and the group must decide on the one(s) on which it will collectively focus its efforts.

You have available to you five RESOURCES. These form the checklist by which a plan can be reviewed for completeness, effectiveness and thorough understanding.

Manpower — How many people do you need? Who will select them? Who will do what? What training do they need? Who will coordinate them?

Money — How much do you have? How much do you really need? Where could you get more? Where could you cut? How will it be allocated? Accounted for?

Materials — What do you need? How will they be selected? Allocated? Maintained? Produced? Accounted for?

Time — How much do you have? How much do you need? Do you have a reserve? Is there a critical time frame on which the plan hinges?

Authority — Who has it? How should it be divided and delegated? How many restraints do you have from the Board?

CONTROLS

The most successful managers are those who have not only thought about what might go wrong, but have actually established the warning system that will tell them in time so that they can do something about it. This is not to say they expect to fail, rather that they are prepared to deal with complications. They have a Plan B.

Every effort should be made to communicate the purpose of controls so that everyone in the group has a clear picture of what is wanted and what is expected. This develops a feeling of security and pride since everyone knows where he stands in relation to the total "game plan". Every individual must know precisely the extent of responsibility, the scope of authority, the standard of performance expected, and the resources available.

Typical controls include:

1. Standards of performance

2. Feedback

3. Personal observation

Standards of performance establish what the expectations are so that variations can be detected. They consist primarily of time schedules, job descriptions and budgets. They provide built-in guides and protection for the individual; they reveal progress of interim goals; provide an opportunity to make corrections before it is too late; and give the satisfaction of knowing you're on the right track.

Feedback is a method of reporting that is basically unstructured. It consists of meetings, oral and written reports and confirming letters, and is founded more on a *feelings* reaction than an intellectual assessment.

Personal observation. The more the manager can personally observe the situation, the easier and earlier adjustment can be made in the plan if it becomes necessary.

ALTERNATE PLANS

All items judged to be both serious and likely should be examined to see what form of alternate planning will produce adequate protection at a reasonable cost. These alternate plans will then be ready to go into effect when your control system shows that performance is not meeting expectations. The basic rule is: the easier it is to recover from something going wrong, the simpler your alternate planning need be. Look for the aspects that really make a difference, and make your detailed alternatives for those. No plan should be considered complete until it has been tested for possible failure and alternate plans have been incorporated.

THE PROCESS

The first two steps of the management process are essentially the planning steps. Step three is the *doing* step, the one in which the entire organization is involved. Management's role turns from one of planning to one of active direction and supervision.

The key to effective execution is well qualified and motivated people. Leadership, rather than management, determines the group's dedication to effort. At this point active vigilance and flexibility are essential. Allow freedom and trust to those responsible for the accomplishment of each task.

Remember – one of the greatest advantages of MBO is its emphasis on *what* is accomplished rather than on *how* a job is done. There must be ample room for individual initiative and innovation within clearly defined work boundaries, as communicated in the monitoring step of planning. These controls must be relatively broad and designed to show deviations from set plans rather than interfere with detailed actions of subordinates.

APPRAISAL

Appraisal is the systematic analysis of all factors that make an organization effective in achieving its objectives. It lays the groundwork for setting new objectives and can be considered a first step as well as a last step. It is a critical tool to insure that the group builds each year on its past successes, formulates new goals and objectives, and thus establishes a constant record of accomplishment.

There are two types of appraisal, internal and external. External appraisal is basically looking outside the organization at all the community factors that might affect the internal planning and execution. Such factors might include available funding, other community efforts, the economic picture, service needs, etc.

Internal appraisal is comprised of three basic elements:

1. Results — did you meet your objective?

2. Resources — what were your results versus resources expended?

3. Management — did MBO work for you?

One failure on the part of many chairmen is their tendency to assess only the negative. Successful groups are built out of assets, not liabilities, and thus a good management appraisal requires a balanced assessment — a review of strengths as well as weaknesses, successes as well as failures, the positive as well as the negative. Criticizing only what has failed or is going wrong, presents a very warped view of reality. This leads management into spending a disproportionate amount of time trying to straighten out faulty resources instead of capitalizing on the resources that are proving effective.

The first element appraised is the results. If the objective has been clearly defined and communicated, the group will continuously assess its position. But there needs to be a final appraisal at the conclusion of the year or event. This becomes an occasion for rewards and group satisfaction. Were all three parts of your original objective met?

When considering resources, look at the results compared with the resources expended. Appraise each of your five resources (3 M's, T-A), manpower, money, materials, time and authority, and evaluate whether each was well utilized. Could you have done the job with less money or would it have been better with more? In achieving the objective, did you burn out the chairman, under-utilize the committee, or rely too heavily on one person? Were your materials adequate? Did you have enough? Too little? Did you have enough time or was the time expended not worth the result? Did you have difficulty delegating authority?

In appraising management, go back through the four steps of the MBO process and evaluate each, for both the positive and the negative. Was the objective clearly defined and communicated to the entire group? Was the objective well stated with a good standard of measurement? Was the objective realistic? Did you have difficulty planning the action? Was the strategy well stated and were the resources realistically allocated? How well did your controls work? Were you adequately warned of possible failure? Did everything proceed on schedule? Did you have difficulty knowing when to step in? Did you have an alternate plan? Was it well developed? Did you need it? This is basically a self-appraisal of how well you managed.

If a group or committee systematically assesses its past performance against these three criteria of *results, resources* and *management,* the strengths and weaknesses, problems and opportunities will quickly become apparent. This will allow you to develop new realistic goals, translate these into definitive, measurable objectives, and thus begin the planning and operating cycle once again. Transitions will be easy and the group can continue independent of the individual members and their respective roles.

You might also consider *making a P.I.E.* To do this, prepare three large newspad sheets — one with *Preserve,* one with *Improve,* and one with *Eliminate.* Consider each element of your project and categorize it. This provides a concise list to work from when formulating new objectives and developing new plans.

P.I.E. EVALUATION

The P.I.E. Evaluation Form has been designed to evaluate the effectiveness of a project or program by considering each of the resources involved (Money, Manpower, Materials, Time and Authority) from an objective stand point. Members of the committee responsible for the activity should be convened soon after completion and asked to consider each resource in terms of whether the approach should be Preserved ("It was perfect!"), Improved ("Good, but next time I'd . . ."), or Eliminated ("Let's not EVER . . . again!").

P.I.E. EVALUATION FORM

	PRESERVE	*IMPROVE*	*ELIMINATE*
(Money)			
(Manpower)			
(Materials)			
(Time)			
(Authority)			

Following the appraisal the group is then set with new directions and future planning can evolve from the successes of the past year. Recommended objectives are created by the outgoing committee for the incoming committee. The new group is then in a position to begin the cycle all over again — setting new objectives based on the suggestions of the previous group.

> *"Never mistake motion for action"*
> Ernest Hemingway

MANAGEMENT BY OBJECTIVES OVERVIEW

An effective manager identifies Key Result Areas and proceeds to specify goals and objectives. For each objective a concept is briefly described and resources allocated, on paper. He communicates these with his co-workers who helped develop them. Realistic alternate plans are specified and controls set up.

Effective management depends on a recognition of the importance of the *approach* as well as the goals and the people. It is a *process* orientation and a commitment to continuity and communication, with clarification that yields success. It is the result of time and effort being invested in the beginning.

This approach forces you to verbalize what you want to do *BEFORE* you jump into planning or are actually doing the job. It insures that programs continue despite yearly turnover, and that everyone understands clearly what is planned.

Goals: Open-ended statements of hopes for the group or committee.

Objectives: Specific and measurable. Objectives have three parts:

1. *What* will be different or accomplished?

2. By when?

3. By what measurement?
   a. *Words to use* — to write, to identify, to solve, to compare, to contrast, to improve, to conduct, to develop, to communicate, to establish, to obtain, to increase, etc.
   b. *Words to avoid* — to know, to be aware, to understand, to appreciate, to believe, to educate (too nonspecific).

Objectives should relate to at least one goal.

Objectives do NOT state *how* you are going to accomplish something but instead, *what* you will accomplish.

Organize For Action: HOW are you going to accomplish your objective? There can be more than one plan of action. This plan is called your CONCEPT (or Strategy). State this briefly — only after your objectives have been agreed upon.

Resources to be allocated:

1. *Money* (budget)

2. *Manpower* (who will be needed for every aspect of plan)

3. *Material*

4. *Time* needed (Schedule)

5. *Authority* (who is responsible for success or failure)

Have an alternate plan.

Establish Controls: This is a check system *established at the outset* to let you know that everything is going as planned. To do this:

1. Set standards of performance — make sure each member knows what is expected of him, what quality is acceptable, and the time schedule to be followed.

2. Provide avenues for feedback — oral or written, such as progress report at a Board or committee meeting.

3. Personal observation — chairman should be available for support and assistance at subcommittee meetings.

Execute the Task: Combine good management with good leadership. Be sensitive to members' feelings, but be strong by being a good manager backed up by a good plan.

Appraise: This can be the end of the objective or the beginning of another objective.

- Did you accomplish what you set out to do?

- Were your resources used effectively or not?

- Did you follow the management process well? (If not, why not?)

- Are you pleased with the results?

- What would you *P*reserve, *I*mprove and *E*liminate?

THE MANAGEMENT PROCESS
GOAL
(Open-ended)

OBJECTIVES
(alterable)
What different?
By When?
How measured?

CONCEPT
(strategy)

ORGANIZE FOR ACTION
(allocation of resources)

1. Manpower: _____

2. Money: _____

3. Material: _____

4. Time: _____

5. Authority: _____

ALTERNATE PLAN

ESTABLISH CONTROLS
(observation-feedback-reporting out)

* * * * EXECUTE THE PLAN * * * *
(do it!)

APPRAISE
(evaluate)

1. Did you achieve your objective? _____
2. Were your resources allocated properly? _____
3. Was the management process used? _____
4. Recommendations for future action: _____
   _____
   _____
   _____

12. Conflict Management

"Let's not fight about this"

I n the interest of harmony, we push aside conflict and ask our members simply to be considerate, or perhaps to try to be understanding. We dread the reaction of strong opinions, threatened egos, strained relationships and lack of objectivity.

When we become open and direct about conflict, situations can become uncomfortable, but without it we have a cold war. At some point you must decide whether to deal with the discomfort of the conflict indefinitely, or to endure a temporary state of high emotion and considerable discomfort while you and your members address the basis of the conflict.

Many view it as a sign of weakness to abandon their stand. What is needed is an attempt to show the individual alternate ways of looking at things in the hope that this may lead to a change in perspective and ultimately a change in attitude. But pave the way for a graceful retreat so the individual may maintain a feeling of self-respect, if compromised.

Rational opposition can usually be countered with facts. However, before trying to change the bias of others be very sure that your own position is based on solid facts. We may actually be dealing with different *values*. Where this is the case, acknowledgement will clear the air, but it is unlikely that the conflict will be resolved.

When dealing with irrational opposition, first express appreciation for the other person's feelings on the subject. Be understanding of the *feelings* if not their rationale. Frequently a person may resist change without being aware of it.

Describe the problem or area of conflict as you see it. Is this how the other person views the situation? Seek to come to an agreement of *what* the problem is. Your conflict may only be perceptual.

FUNCTIONS OF CONFLICT

All resistance and conflict need not be seen as negative. Each can serve a very useful function. It can:

- Cause the leader to clarify more sharply the purpose of the proposed change and the results to be sought.
- Point out the need for a greater sense of 'team' within the group itself.
- Disclose the inadequacy of the current problem solving or decision-making techniques.
- Bring to light the weakness in the communication process and the flow of information.

To diagnose conflict, identify:

A. The nature of the difference
   Is the disagreement based on:
   1. facts?
   2. values?
   3. goals?
   4. methods?
B. The underlying differences
   1. Is the individual influenced by his *role?*
   2. Do the individuals have access to diversified information?
   3. Do they have a different perspective of the same information?

TASK VS. PROCESS

It is regrettable that most of our dealings with organizations, or affiliations with Boards, are approached from the standpoint of a *task* to be accomplished. We have a common interest (the blind, the museum, the Scouts, the school), but we allow little time for consideration of the *process*. We invest our energies in making something happen without recognizing that the outcome and feelings of satisfaction will be affected by the *process* involved in making it happen. If everyone is in perpetual conflict we may still reap thousands of dollars ... but along the way we may lose our most reliable and productive members out of frustration and discontent.

To minimize resistance and conflict there are several things a volunteer, particularly a leader, can do. Listed below are five points to consider.

- Think consciously about your problem solving technique
- Maximize the participation of your members in *all* decisions
- Encourage imagination and creativity
- Open up communication by helping everyone to feel at ease
- Keep an open flow of information

MANAGING CONFLICT

To *manage* conflict you must be willing to alter your approach to dealing with conflict. To do this first identify how you are currently handling conflict.

Do you:

- Complain — or do you suggest reasonable change?
- Shut out others — or do you ask for and give feedback on conflict issues?
- Stand by your guns — or are you willing to consider compromise?
- Make presumptions about other people's positions — or do you seek clarification?
- Label people — or do you stick to the issues instead of the personalities?
- Continually cite what happened last week, last month or last year — or do you concentrate on what is happening now?

BARRIERS TO CONFRONTATION

Many times conflict is not openly dealt with because the parties involved find that *excuses not to* deal with it outweigh *reasons for* confrontation. Individuals are reluctant to leave their "comfort zone", even though it may mean solving the problem. It involves "risk-taking", a scary thing for many people.

Some of the barriers to open confrontation include:

- Insufficient time to work things out
- Feeling that volunteers, especially chairmen, should not express negative feelings

- Personal concept of your role within the group
- Public image concerns
- Desire to avoid hurting others' feelings
- Fear of one's own vulnerability to the other's conflict tactics
- Fear that your efforts will not be reciprocated

Once you have considered these barriers and have recognized the need to make a change in yourself, or to take a stand or risk, then you are in a position to manage conflict. Conflict really shouldn't be avoided; it should be acknowledged and where possible, resolved.

STRATEGIES

A difference of opinion need not be viewed as a conflict area. *Perception* decides whether or not there is a conflict. When we decide there is in fact a conflict, there are at least five identifiable strategies for dealing with it. These include:

1. *Competition*   Useful in emergencies, when an unpopular decision has to be implemented

2. *Avoidance*   Useful when you perceive it is best to leave well enough alone, to buy time and when damage caused by confrontation will outweigh benefits

3. *Accommodation*   Use when the issue means more to others, when harmony is seen as more important, when you are open to a solution other than your own

4. *Compromise*   Use to achieve a temporary settlement, when time is of the essence, when you are working from mutually exclusive goals

5. *Collaboration*   Problem Solving. Use when concerns are too great to compromise, when solution affects long range trends, when the decision will greatly affect all involved

PROBLEM SOLVING

This final strategy is the most permanent way of dealing with conflict, and it takes the most effort, with the cooperation of all. It involves a problem solving approach which leads to a win/win solution. The steps include:

1. *Diagnosis* of the kind of conflict
2. *Initiation* of a confrontation a) Identify the tangible effects the conflict has; b) Avoid putting the participants on the defensive; c) Criticize only the situation, never the people
3. *Active Listening* a) Hear the other's point of view; b) Clarify by restating the view of others to assure your understanding; c) Have regard for the feelings and words of others
4. *Problem Solving* itself is the final step, begun only when all agree there is a situation (a problem) which needs change

For suggestions about productive and effective problem solving see chapter 9 titled "Problem Solving".

NEGOTIATING

> "Knowledge is the skill to take something apart,
> and wisdom is the ability to put it back together
> again"

If we view conflict management as a skill, we should consider *negotiating* a fine art. If your group is faced with negotiating, for example, for a percentage of the profit from a commercial booth at your carnival — send your best negotiator. Some of us are simply too willing to accept *any* offer. Others are capable of working out an arrangement which is still acceptable to all involved . . . and better than the first offer.

With this in mind, consider the following points important in negotiating. Your awareness of these will put you ahead from the start.

1. People are different — they have different needs, and they perceive things differently. Present your case in a manner that relates to the others' needs.

2. Make things personal — of course you are representing your organization or group, but the point you want to make is that *you* are counting on this individual.

3. Negotiate privately — don't set out to accomplish change in a public situation where an individual is apt to be more concerned with defending his stand or saving face.

4. Only propose an ultimatum if you are in a position to back it up (such as never renting their facility again) and if the other party believes you will back it up.

5. Deal face to face — it is easier to say no on the phone or in a letter. Don't give your opposition this advantage.

6. Always initiate any call or meeting — *you* have the advantage of coming prepared and setting the terms, including the ultimate deadline.

7. Always initiate the contract or memo — *you* establish the terms.

8. Never hesitate to ask for help from the opposition, to understand or to clarify. Get them involved in a collaborative effort and attempt to diminish the competitiveness of the environment.

9. Consider timing — look for the best time, not just any time, to negotiate. This can affect your prospect for success.

10. Remember there are always options. Make the choice. *You* be the one in charge of the situation.

When negotiating, your influence is related to the extent to which you share open communication, as well as the degree of trust established. The relationships people have within a group greatly affect not only their actual power and influence, but how much they perceive they have. For this reason, a healthy organization will invest in developing trust among its members very early in their association.

The obstacles to effective negotiation are reduced considerably if concern has been demonstrated for each member as an individual, and by keeping open the doors of communication.

In fact, the implication is that to effectively negotiate with dissenters your first concern should be with the inter-personal relationships. Unless people are willing to let down their guards, and at the same time feel safe and unintimidated, they are in no position to negotiate differences objectively.

Communication skills and a warm, caring feeling of team are primary elements in an effective organization or Board. Once these have been established a group is in a position to set about *negotiating*.

Competencies seen by professionals as important to negotiating, and influencing others, include:

- A degree of personal security (poise and confidence)
- Situational skill (ability to perceive complexities)
- Independence and courage of judgment (ability to substantiate claims, and stand strongly for a position)
- Ability to abstract and conceptualize
- Mental flexibility (ability to adjust and to add new dimensions)
- Tolerence for ambiguity (not pressured to find immediate solutions)
- Ability to analyze and synthesize (to see relationships)

A quick glance at the list above will tell you why you may often fail at your efforts to influence change. The parties involved do not have the needed skills to negotiate!

Regrettably, many of the difficulties faced by non-profit agencies revolve around inner turmoil, ineffective inter-personal relationships. This simply points to the need to be as concerned about HOW you do what you do as you are with WHAT you do.

Considerable effort should be spent on the *process*. Annual orientation of group members can establish the tone for the year. If it is approached in a positive, constructive, organized manner the message will be, "We want to work with you, we care about you, we're glad you care about us".

Then, if and when any problems develop, you are in a far better position to persuade. A win/win solution is possible, but only when an atmosphere of understanding and caring have been established. Organizations will only be effective when they devote as much attention to the process as to the products of their efforts.

PREPARATION FOR NEGOTIATION

There are several essential considerations when approaching a negotiating situation; these include:

- Know what you want
- Be prepared with facts
- Know what your opposition is
- Prepare your presentation, point by point
- Anticipate reactions
- Develop an approach in tune with the other's capacity to understand and appreciate
- Develop a climate of cooperation
- Remain open to the feelings of the other
- Help the other to develop a better position
- Allow the other to save face
- Steer away from an approach which will incite defense mechanisms
- Establish respect for the other's self esteem
- Consider timing and method

STEPS IN NEGOTIATING

To be an effective negotiator, learn to listen to what the other person wants and needs, and to appeal to these needs. Welcome objections, and show appreciation for the other person's point of view (even if you do not agree).

Step 1: Phrase your proposal in such a way as to assure agreement to several points at the beginning. ("I think we can both agree there is a problem, and *something* really must be done.", for example).

Step 2: Seek to remove obstacles to agreement by developing a sense of progress. ("It seems to me we both agree the x,w,z.")

Step 3: Create a common sense of flexibility and appreciation for the other's adaptability. ("I appreciate that you see my point here, and I agree that x,y,z.)

KEYS TO EFFECTIVE NEGOTIATION

Whenever there seems to be a need to negotiate, with co-workers or other community people, there are several key points to remember. The following will help assure ultimate satisfaction by both parties:

- Remain open to the other's point of view

- Avoid overselling

- Stand strong in your position (don't apologize for it)

- Let the buck stop here

- Exercise patience

- Be gracious and courteous

- Emphasize the positive

- Avoid arrogance, belittling, ridicule, and sarcasm

If it would be helpful, the points listed above could be reviewed by the parties involved just prior to entering into the negotiating process. This chart could be kept at the table or on the wall for reference to assure that each is approaching the situation on workable terms.

> "Criticism is like surgery. It always hurts and at times it can be fatal. It requires careful preparation by both physician and patient. The doctor must be calm and steady, and the patient must be willing and ready."
>
> Dr. Haim Ginott

Dr. Haim Ginott recommended that we learn to *respond*, instead of to react. This is very hard to do when emotions are high and trouble brewing. However, when we *react* we are reflecting our own experiences and feelings, we are behaving because of what *we* know. Taking time to calmly *respond* allows you to get into the other person's feelings.

Conflict should neither be welcomed nor avoided. However, it is to be expected. Conflict is bound to occur in any group of people with great concern for issues. Conflict reminds us that we are human. Solutions are only possible when conflict is acknowledged and dealt with openly, with the help of all concerned. It is a challenge, a hurdle, but it need not be an insurmountable barrier to success.

The ability to confront (specific issues) depends on several factors:

- A sense of significance in the relationship
- An interset in saving the relationship
- A feeling of self worth
- A belief that you will be *heard*
- A clear idea of how you 'feel' and what you want
- Knowledge that the other person cares about changing things
- An open, honest, trusting base
- A commitment to something greater than the two individuals

If any of the above points are not established it is an indication that this item must first be delt with and discussed. Without a healthy relationship confrontation simply ignites defenses and encourages anger.

A few reasons why people *avoid* confrontation, include:

- *I don't want to hurt the other person.*
  The intent is to make things better. Sometimes it hurts to hear that we are not doing what we think we are (see page 108). But this hurt allows for the possibility of finding a solution and easing the pain.

- *If you can't say anything nice you shouldn't say anything at all.*
  If said in private, and with the interest in making things better, it ought to be said.

- *I'll just sound like a nag.*
  A nag speaks only of the problem. In effective confrontation a solution is proposed or negotiated.

- *I don't want the other person mad at me.*
  The truth hurts and sometimes makes people mad. Be sure to deal first with creating a climate in which emotions are calm.

- *Nothing will change.*
  As long as you believe it won't, it won't. Change your attitude and it just may. The only way to find out is to try. It surely won't if you don't bring up the issue.

13. Self Assessment/ Group Assessment

"Where Are We Going?"

"It is your *ATTITUDE*, not your *APTITUDE*,
which determines your *ALTITUDE*"

The Reverend Jesse Jackson

M ake your life an adventure in which you are proud of your role. That's a fine goal. And, in good management by objective style, periodically evaluate your adventure so as to stay on course and to give yourself both an opportunity to avoid pitfalls and a chance for personal praise. It's just as important that *you* view what you are doing as productive and positive, as to be recognized by others for this. Take time to evaluate your progress; reward yourself. By doing this, you will strengthen your identity and be less vulnerable to the effects of invalid criticism by others.

This may require simply a change in perspective. Try altering your view of those things which you conceive as problems. If seen as challenges, they take on a whole new light. It is also important to remember that yesterday is behind you. I hope you learned from it — but don't dwell on it and don't let it get you down. Work on today. Live now! This is your only chance to experience this moment. Why not make the very most of it. Live it to the fullest. Let all senses be alive.

"The quality, not the longevity, of one's life is what is important."
Martin Luther King, Jr.

Develop a mental picture of the person you would like to be. It's the first step in becoming that person. Focus your efforts on activities within your area of competence. Consider what your strengths are and what exceeds your ability. Be honest and realistic. Also, your tasks shouldn't be in conflict with your values, or you're apt to find unhappiness ahead.

GETTING TO KNOW YOURSELF

We get a certain picture of ourselves by the responses others make to us. If we choose to ignore these, we've learned nothing. But if we take notes, we're ahead. For example, are you never elected to office but perpetually appointed "chairman of the world"? Perhaps it is because you are a manager rather than a leader. There is a difference, and knowing the difference can set you on the track of a more satisfying volunteer path.

Leaders are born, but *leadership* can be learned. Leaders are people with a sensitivity to others who recognize feelings and respond from emotions. There are many volunteer slots absolutely perfect for a person like this, including right hand to a chairman. They can serve as a buffer, much as they work well in vice-presidential slots in the business world, tempering tensions and emotions between directors and staff.

Leaders are those wonderful people with charisma who inspire others by the smiles on their faces or the twinkle in their eyes. They're the Pied Pipers of the world, and with positive factors working on their side, they turn out to be the John F. Kennedys of the world instead of the Hitlers. They are elected to positions of authority.

Managers, on the other hand, are those appointed to office. They are recognized by others as having considerable skill and ability in dealing with tasks. They have analytical problem-solving minds and work from intellect — what the facts tell them.

The skills of management can also be learned. Leaders can learn to become good managers by applying tools which help facilitate the process of accomplishing tasks. Unfortunately, it is much harder to learn to become a leader, but not impossible. It involves learning to be sensitive to others.

Management can be seen as a science, one of getting things done by allocating resources with the focus on results. Leadership is the art of motivating people to do things. The focus is on the people.

As volunteers we can take an objective look at ourselves and say, "My title may be Girl Scout *leader*, but by this definition I'm really much more of a task-oriented person, and, acknowledging that, I will seek to work at a level and in an area where such skills are essential. I'll let those with a greater sensitivity to people handle those positions that require leadership skills."

The concept of "Flying up" with your Scouts is potentially as irrational as the Peter Principle in business: "In a hierarchy every employee tends to rise to his level of incompetence." As long as we're performing magnificently as a Brownie leader, planning, organizing, executing, why should we move up to Junior Scouts? This is where sensitivity to the girls' needs and abilities is far greater and where opportunities for planning and organizing should be passed on to the girls. It may frustrate you if the job isn't accomplished to your satisfaction. It may also frustrate the scouts if you continue to do for them and offer few opportunities for them to learn to plan and organize for themselves.

This is not to say that no one out there could do both. Just take a minute first to appraise yourself, to assess your skills, abilities and temperament. Are you equally cut out for this opportunity as you were for the last? Moving in isn't always moving up if the requirements of the job are alien to your abilities. By the same token, for some, being overall chairman — orchestrating the activities of others — may be far easier than the responsibilities of a single committee chairmanship, if it's the wrong one.

Volunteering should be fun. It should leave you with good feelings. There is a flexibility in terms of time commitment and requirements not available in the working world. Many must endure positions for security reasons, but in the volunteer community, we can say "no" to a position that will not bring us satisfaction. It's better for everyone that we do say "no" to volunteer opportunities that we really won't take on with enthusiasm. They will be better done by someone else.

SELF ASSESSMENT
*"A man has to live with himself, and he should see to it
that he always has good company."* C. E. Hughes

How often have your heard, "Today is the beginning of the rest of your life?" It's true. Start now! But start with a plan, one built *after* you have had a good look at yourself.

What do *you* want out of life? What challenges do you thrive on? What mountains do you want to climb? What skills and talents do you possess which will help assure success?

To help you to focus on how you behave as a volunteer, try selecting words, from the following choices, which seem best to describe you:

I.	II.	III.	IV.
forceful	enthusiastic	systematic	patient
adventurous	outgoing	diplomatic	loyal
demanding	emotional	conscientious	stable
daring	sociable	conventional	team oriented
decisive	generous	analytical	calm
self-assured	convincing	sensitive	deliberate
competitive	trusting	accurate	passive

If you identified terms primarily from column I, you are probably good at initiating new ideas, getting results, making decisions, solving problems and taking authority.

Those terms listed in column II reflect individuals who tend to be good at motivating, entertaining, generating enthusiasm, interacting with others and offering assistance.

If, on the other hand, you selected more words from the third column, you are apt to be better at following directions, working with specific assignments, being diplomatic and doing critical thinking.

Those in the last column describe individuals who generally demonstrate patience and understanding, are loyal, act as good listeners, can work with few new challenges and are good at concentrating.

With this information as a springboard, start a page and begin to describe yourself, as you see yourself.

Now, using the same lists, consider whether you might also identify areas which are difficult for you. For example, those who select more descriptive words from the first column may find they are not very cautious, or good at calculating risks. They may be uncomfortable in a protected environment, or researching and deliberating.

Those of you who chose more words from column II may have trouble working alone, or just with ideas. You may have difficulty concentrating, or seeking out facts and considering new ideas. These are just considerations, intended to get you focusing on how you function.

The serene, complacent volunteer, of the third column, may have difficulty with critical thinking, with acting independently, delegating or making decisions, especially unpopular ones.

The patient loyal workers described in column IV may have trouble with change, or working under pressure, with too many expectations, or where considerable physical energy is needed.

With this in mind, you may want to look for positions which I. have considerable freedom, with prestige and challenge, or II. have many social activities, with little need for detail work and allow you to share ideas, or III. assure security and a sense of being a part of the group in a comfortable, familiar setting, or IV. provides traditional procedures in a designated area of activity, where appreciation is shown.

We all have qualities and needs represented in each area listed — but tend to be more like one set of descriptive words than another.

VOLUNTEER OPPORTUNITIES

Once you have begun to clarify for yourself just what sort of a worker you are, consider the requirements of the challenge being offered you. This may change annually as you are asked to wear still another hat from one year to the next. Each job offers different challenges, and you may be equipped to deal with some better than with others.

Consider your newest volunteer opportunity. Must you:

- Initiate new program or ideas?
- Be prepared to make unpopular decisions?
- Display diplomacy?
- Deal with complete strangers, perhaps in a coalition?
- Do future planning?
- Deal exclusively with detail work?
- Take calculated risks?
- Organize the efforts of others?
- Endure basically boring work, filled with repetition?
- Be responsible for motivating others?
- Follow to the letter plans developed by someone else?
- Develop the independence of those working with you?
- Provide skill training to new members?
- Deal with people problems?
- Be responsible for public speaking?
- Endure perpetual change and constant interruption?
- Be responsible for developing policy?
- Patiently follow specific instructions?
- Integrate new programs into an existing system?

Just what is being asked of you? Do you have a job description and a clear idea of what is expected of you by those who suggested you take on the new task?

Beyond all this, what do you really want from your involvement in a volunteer organization? Why do you belong? Make a list. Now rank these reasons. Look at your list again. This time rank each item in terms of the availability of opportunity to meet each need through this organization and this paticular challenge.

Another exercise you might try, to come to know yourself better, is to pretend you're fishing and that the potential catch includes:

wisdom	happiness	faith	popularity
health	fame	honesty	courage
love	power	friends	skill
creativity	excitement	beauty	wealth

You've had a good day and you have caught the five fish you'd hoped to catch. Check these. However, while you doze off on the bank of the river, two get away. Mark out these two from your catch. Then, along comes your best friend, and he's hungry, you give him one of your fish (cross it off). And, while you talk, a cat sneaks up and runs off with another fish — leaving you with just one. Which is it? It is probably what you value most ...what are you doing to see to it that your time is spent in activities which will provide you with this?

The world needs differences. We balance one another. Some people are simply better equipped to handle and derive satisfaction from different challenges. The trick is to determine in advance what *you* need and thrive on. Don't say "yes" just to please. To really get the most out of your volunteer experience, you have needs that must be satisfied.

To have a really successful committee or project, we need someone who will generate new ideas, a marketing person to promote them, dependable workers to follow through, and a detail person to keep us on track and within necessary guidelines. You probably could fill one of these slots better than another.

QUESTIONS FOR SELF-ANALYSIS

The following questions have been designed to get you thinking — to take time out to focus on why you are doing what you are doing, and in some cases to consider how you might improve the situation.

1. Why am I volunteering?

2. What are my strengths as a volunteer?

3. What are my weaknesses as a volunteer?

4. How can I measure my effectiveness as a volunteer?

5. To what degree are my volunteer activities planned?

6. Do I allow for individual differences among committee members in my volunteer activities?

7. What are my objectives for each volunteer activity?

8. How can I measure the accomplishment of my volunteer activities?

9. Am I good at: (1) lecturing, (2) demonstrating, or (3) facilitating activities?

10. What is my favorite activity? Why?

11. Do I show flexibility as a volunteer?

12. What skills are most important in my volunteer activities?

13. Are there any skills I would like to acquire? How could I gain this skill or knowledge?

14. What sort of volunteer do I enjoy working with most?

15. What response or involvement do I expect from volunteer efforts?

16. In what way does my volunteer effort make a difference to others?

Additionally, you might ask yourself whether the volunteer challenge you most enjoyed . . .

- Called upon skill or knowledge

- Allowed you control over how and what you did

- Put you in a position of authority

- Gave you a chance to help others

- Increased your feeling of self worth

- Provided an adventure or challenge

- Was cause for recognition from others

- Gave you a chance to learn and grow

Knowing what factors are important to you can help you to select volunteer opportunities which are most apt to meet your needs.

ASSESSING OURSELVES AS LEADERS

Once you accept a leadership position and have thought about the kind of leader you'd like to become, you might do an assessment of your present capabilities. The chart below may help to give you an idea of how you view yourself.

Leadership Assessment	Most of the time	Some of the time	Need to improve
In my leadership roles I see myself as able to:			
1. Sense the attitudes and feelings of myself and others			
2. Develop leadership in members of my group			
3. Delegate responsibility to the appropriate persons			
4. Tolerate differences of opinion			
5. Find creative solutions to problems			
6. Establish work assignments			
7. Face mistakes, accept responsibility, and move on			
8. Be flexible			
9. Identify and analyze group problems			
10. Bring out the best efforts in others			
11. Seek help from other qualified people			
12. Evaluate myself and others fairly			
How could you capitalize on your strengths? What could you do to improve in your areas of weakness?			

Here are other self-disclosure exercises. These are useful to you only to the extent that you learn more about yourself and become conscious of the qualities revealed.

VALUES RELATING TO WORK	Interest	Independence	Self-expression	Service	Leadership	Social Relationships	Reward	Achievement	Recognition	Accomplishment	Variety	Security
1.												
2.												
3.												
4.												
5.												
6.												
7.												
8.												
9.												
10.												
Total												

In the 10 spaces, list paid or unpaid work, programs, projects, or activities that you have done because they were important to you.

Check each of the columns which seem appropriate for each of the positions you have listed on the form (definitions on following page). Total the responses in each column on the value sheet.

Through this you can begin to determine the strength of your values as related to your work or volunteer activities. Suggested next step:

On a fresh sheet of paper, write a paragraph or two on each of the following:

What I have learned about myself and my work values

What work value emerges the most? The least? Why?

VALUES RELATING TO WORK

INTEREST: Any activity you did because you really liked doing it. This is one of your special interests, and you find it stimulating.

INDEPENDENCE: An activity you liked because you could work alone, without a lot of supervision and direction from others. You like the feeling of being independent.

SELF-EXPRESSION: Any activity which allowed you to use your natural talent or ability, because you could express who you really are and what you do well.

SERVICE: Anything you did because it had meaning for others or because it was for another person's benefit. You have a need to help others, and like to do a good and useful job wherever you are needed.

LEADERSHIP: Activities you did because you like to challenge your leadership abilities. You enjoy planning and organizing and get a feeling of satisfaction from knowing that you can direct and supervise the activities of others.

SOCIAL RELATIONSHIPS: Any activity which drew you to involvement because your greatest pleasure is doing things with others.

REWARD: Activities you did because you expected to receive a reward of some kind, such as money, approval or a special privilege.

ACHIEVEMENT: An activity you did because advancement and growth are important to you. You like to do things well and to do your best when you do something.

RECOGNITION: Any activity you did because recognition of your work by others is important to you. You like being respected, having prestige, and receiving approval for what you do.

ACCOMPLISHMENT: An activity which comes to completion because of your involvement, such as a program presented or project put into action. You are particularly task oriented and like measurable results.

VARIETY: An activity you did because you like to do new things. You don't like routine or repetitious work.

SECURITY: Any activity you did because you felt comfortable doing it. You were familiar with this and you like to do the things you find easy to do.

Based on material in *How To Decide — A Workbook For Women*, by Nellie Tumlin Scholz, Judith Sosebee Prince, & Gordon Miller. Avon Books, 1975

DATA, PEOPLE AND THINGS

The following is one final activity you might try to determine a productive direction for your volunteer efforts.

- **Working with Data**

  Check one of the 3 choices listed below

  - ☐ 1. I prefer work that is uncomplicated and easy to learn. I don't mind using information in a simple way if it doesn't require too much mental energy.
  - ☐ 2. I like keeping track of and working with information in an orderly way. I prefer having others responsible for directing this work.
  - ☐ 3. I enjoy organizing and administering information, as well as planning and developing ideas and new ways of doing things.

- **Involvement with People**

  Check one of the three choices listed below

  - ☐ 1. I prefer involvement with information or things, though I don't mind a minimal interaction with people.
  - ☐ 2. I like organizing and inspiring other people to do things.
  - ☐ 3. I enjoy entertaining people and being the key person in a group.

- **Dealing with Things**

  Check one of the three choices listed below

  - ☐ 1. I prefer little involvement with things. If I must work with things I prefer uncomplicated, easy to learn procedures.
  - ☐ 2. I enjoy running equipment with care and efficiency, but I prefer that someone else have responsibility for directing the work.
  - ☐ 3. I enjoy using my hands to work with intricate tools and machines, and I like to be responsible for complex equipment which I understand.

A check in Box 1 indicates low interest in Data, People or Things. A check in box 2 refers to a moderate interest and Box 3 a high or considerable interest.

Once you have determined whether your highest interest lies with Data, People or Things you are in a better position to select volunteer opportunities which will satisfy you and meet the needs of your organization. The success ratio is greatly improved if volunteers commit themselves to activities which meet their inner needs.

After you have considered the options listed above, you might find that you have a high interest in more than one area. This is lucky for you and your organization. It implies that you bring considerable enthusiasm to a variety of activities. To select the best avenue for you at this time consider the ramifications of each specific opportunity offered. Does it fit your time schedule? Is it in a location that suits you? Would you enjoy the co-workers? Is the environment one in which you would thrive?

GROUP ASSESSMENT

The real reason for doing any sort of Group Assessment is to remedy problems and plot a successful course for the future.

We have heard the term "management by crisis" applied to business. Regrettably, the same is often true in many organizations. It comes from the failure to identify trends, assess interests, set realistic objectives, and do reasonable future planning.

When discussing future planning it is important to focus on your resources and build on your strengths. When planning for the future of your organization, several key points should be considered:

- The needs and goals of the general membership, not just your Board

- The needs of those you serve

- The priorities of the members, as well as of the community

- The potential resources available to you, from the community at large

- The implications of major areas of change, such as technology, Women's Lib, and the environment

- The manpower, within your group, available and interested in being actively involved

- The trends of the community at large, as well as the economy

- Remain flexible, and view your task as *on-going*

Future planning requires a real commitment to the organization or agency and a sincere interest in assuring the success of its programs and projects in a world where everything is changing. It means having a positive outlook and a belief in the ability of members and staff to prepare for this new world with its new challenges. It means caring about the people who will make it happen, and having to deal with the obstacles as well as the opportunities. It means involving everyone affected by the decisions in the decision making process.

NEEDS ASSESSMENT

If your group is going to remain active and continue to be motivated, it is essential to periodically do some sort of "Needs Assessment". Members will not perform at their optimum level if their needs are not being met. With this in mind, before planning for the coming year, consider developing a questionnaire that will help assess the feelings of those you hope to involve and satisfy.

For example:

- Are they happy with the basic purpose of your group? (If not, is it time to reconsider your reason for being?)

- Do they like the format of your meetings, the frequency as well as the time and location? (If not, what would be their preference?)

- Is the structure of your organization workable, considering current challenges? (If not, how might you reorganize to be more effective?)

- Do your members have the skills needed to perform the tasks expected of them? (If not, would they be receptive to skill training and who could present this?)

- Do they feel they, as members, have a voice in the decisions being made? (If not, what is their objection and how could the situation be improved?)

- Is there adequate communication? (If not, what changes could be made to assure that those in need of information have prompt, first hand access to it?)

- Are the lines of communication and authority clear and acceptable? (If not, what changes would bring about greater satisfaction?)

- What are the personal motives of your members for belonging? (Are your programs and activities planned with these in mind?)

Do you ever wonder how your members view your organization? Why is it that so few seem to do so much? You might consider developing a questionnaire to have your members fill out at one of your meetings (ideally your largest). To assure that you get input from everyone, especially those who so often are not there, you could mail out the form (with a stamped, self-addressed return envelope) to those absent.

The following are two sets of questions from which you could build a workable questionnaire.

Part I

1. Personal characteristics of your members:
   a. Age
   b. Marital status
   c. Age of youngest child
   d. Years with the group
   e. Employed? Full__ Part time__
   f. Board experience (with the group)
2. What are they looking for with membership in your group?
3. What have they liked about their association with the group?
   a. Most?
   b. Least?
4. How do they feel the community sees your group?
5. Have they enjoyed the opportunities provided by your group?
6. Do they tend to feel:
   a. Over worked?_____
   b. Overlooked?_____
7. Have the meeting times been:
   a. Good for their schedule?_____
   b. In conflict?_____
8. Has the frequency of the meetings been reasonable?
9. Is the location of the meetings convenient?
10. Do they feel a part of the decision making?

Part II

This section is designed to have members consider the importance, to them, of 8 items regarding their feelings and involvement with your organization. In the portion designed A they are to list the importance of these factors and in B the degree of satisfaction they find through your current structure.

A				Part II	B			
Extremely Important	Important	Of Some Importance	No Difference	GROUP ASSESSMENT	Completely Satisfied	Could Be Better	Barely Satisfied	Unsatisfied
				1. Feeling needed by others				
				2. Working with interesting people				
				3. Chance to improve myself				
				4. Having a chance to serve as a Board member				
				5. Being active in the community				
				6. Doing interesting things & getting away from routine				
				7. Developing friendships				
				8. Doing specific tasks which are of interest to me				

If your group numbers under 50, many open-ended questions could be used. However, if larger, this would become time consuming to tabulate.

It is usually a good idea to assure your group that their answers will be anonymous, and to remind them of the importance of being completely honest.

Finally, before you ask that they take the time to share their views with you be sure that you (the Board) are prepared to say in what manner you will use the information.

Are you willing to re-schedule your meetings if this turns out to be an area of complaint? Would you add internal social events if there is great interest? Could you develop a tool to determine areas of interest (such as a nominating questionnaire) if your members feel overlooked? The members need to be assured that there is a real possibility for change.

With tools such as these there must be obvious follow-up. The information, and time spent to share it, must be acknowledged. After this the information should be used to re-establish your purpose, policies or program so that the needs of the participants are being met. Group members need to know they are being heard and appreciated.

GROUP ASSESSMENT ACTIVITIES

Organizational Activities
(To clarify expectations and wishes of the group)

Step 1. On a prepared form, have each member answer the following:
    a. List some of the things you hope this group might try to do this year.
    b. List 3 things you hope the group will bring to you (what you hope to gain from membership).
    c. List what you feel the group should expect of its members.
    d. List what special skills, leadership or services you feel you can contribute.

Step 2. Divide into pairs and let each individual interview a partner, sharing their responses to the questions above.

Step 3. Separate the pairs and re-group to repeat step 2.

Step 4. On a large newssheet compile the data from the entire group to determine how widely each feeling is shared.

To Reveal The Unspoken Goals
(of the members)

Step 1. Give each member 3 cards designated A, B, and C.

Step 2. Ask each member to answer (anonymously) the following questions on the appropriate card:

a) Why did you join this group?

b) What do you personally hope to gain from your membership?

c) What do you believe to be the goal of this group?

Step 3. Stack all of the cards by letter and divide into three groups. Each group is then asked to review the cards, and on newsprint, compile a list of the ideas from their cards.

Step 4. Review the three lists as a group, share feelings, acknowledge differences and realize that personal needs will change.

Step 5. This is a good starting point for zeroing in on agreement as to what, in fact, are the current goals of the group.

To Help Members Develop Clear Goals

In advance of the meeting ask members to complete the following statements that have been prepared for them:

a. I joined this group because-

b. This group aims to-

c. I wish this group would-

d. I want our group to become-

At the meeting review the responses with the participants. On a flip chart the ideas can be recorded before the group. Upon completion, discuss how well you are doing and what you could be doing to more generally satisfy the members.

It would not be necessary to try all of the above activities. However, if you are truly interested in doing a Group Assessment you could seriously consider making time for one of them.

SKILL BANK

Having members fill out a questionnaire revealing their skills can be valuable when it comes time to slate officers and man projects and committees. It is also a way of assessing individual needs and areas of interest, and involving volunteers in activities, environments & time frames of *their* choosing.

The following represents information you might find useful.

- PERSONAL DATA

  Name, address, phone, your schooling, spouse's name and occupation, dates of children's birth

- EMPLOYMENT STATUS
  Full or part time, employer, address, phone, position
- COMMUNITY INVOLVEMENT
  Organizations and positions
- SKILLS
  Clerical
  Public contact (research, interviewing, public speaking, training, telephoning)

  Media communication (writing copy, working with T.V., radio, papers)
  art (lettering, layout, drawing)

  Organizational (setting objectives, conducting meetings, planning, motivating others, knowledge of bylaws or parliamentary procedure)

  Ways and means (developing project ideas, writing proposals, preparing budgets, knowledge of community resources)

  Research and education (research design, writing questionnaires, dealing with statistics, key punch, computer program)

  Evaluating and reporting
  Cultural arts (acting, crafts, photography, dancing, drama, music)
  Special areas (i.e. working with children, elderly, handicapped, etc.)
  Languages (country?, reading, speaking, writing)
- REASONS FOR JOINING THIS GROUP
- POSITIONS HELD IN THIS ORGANIZATION
- IN WHAT CAPACITY WOULD YOU LIKE THIS ORGANIZATION TO BE INVOLVED IN THE FUTURE?
- IN WHAT CAPACITY WOULD YOU LIKE TO SERVE? (president, nominating, fund raising chairman, docent, etc.)
- VOLUNTEER INVOLVEMENT
  Types of activities available, time slots & environmental settings

Should you choose to develop a skill bank, the material outlined above can be set in questionnaire form. It is important to leave adequate space to fully respond to each section, AND, to *use* the information filed in a Skill Bank.

When designing a questionnaire there are a number of different approaches you can use. Each technique produces a different kind of data. The following outline reviews points for gathering productive data. See Appendix for how to design a questionnaire.

GATHERING PRODUCTIVE DATA

This kind of response	results in *This kind of data*	*Advantages*	*Disadvantages*
1. Fill-in-the-blank	Nominal	Less Biasing, greater response flexibility	Harder to score, social bias affects response & interpretation
2. Scaled	Interval (Quantitative)	Easy to score	Time consuming; can be biasing
3. Ranking procedure	Ordinal	Easy to score Forces respondent to make choice	Difficult to complete
4. Checklist	Nominal	Easy to score and to respond	Fewer options provides less data

Examples of each:

1. Looking at your present situation, what do you expect to be doing five years from now?_____

2. How do you feel about the proposed change in our group's age limit:
   strongly approve approve uncertain disapprove strongly disapprove

3. Please rank the following proposed fund raisers in order of preference to you. (1=most interesting, 5=least interesting, (<u>Rank</u> only 4)

(Try to	Black tie Ball	_____
include	Cabaret	_____
all the	Las Vegas night	_____
possibilities)	Art auction	_____
	Rummage sale	_____
	Christmas boutique	_____
	Other (please specify)	_____

4. My current employment status is:

    _____(1) work full time (paid employment)
    _____(2) work part time (paid employment)
    _____(3) no paid employment

— Notice *none* of the above features a "paragraph answer" — that kind of "soft information" is very hard to analyze on a large scale.

— Pertinent questions: How would I enter the information on a computer card?
How would I *code* it?

(based on material in *Conducting Educational Research,* by Bruce Tuckman)

QUESTIONS FOR CONSIDERATION

The answers to these questions should be used to plan for the future.

- Are your needs being met?
            If so why:_____
            If not, why not?_____

- Do you feel comfortable with co-workers?

- Are you proud to be a part of this organization?

- How did you happen to join?

- How long do you expect to be involved?

- Are expectations for your efforts clear?

- Do you feel challenged?

-             appreciated?

- Do you have the resources you need to do the job?

- What do you tell others about your association with this group?

VOLUNTEER EXIT REVIEW

One way to determine just how effective your volunteer program is involves an Exit Review. Some volunteers will simply drop by the wayside, others will formally resign, and others will leave a cloud of dust and dismay in their wake. To intercept factors which are *agency-caused reasons for leaving* a group would be wise to solicit an Exit Review. This is best done in privacy by filling out an Exit Review form.

A form such as the following can be sent, with a self-addressed stamped envelope to the "dearly departed". Honesty is important. It must be pursued in a way that allows the former volunteer to tell you truthfully why he or or she left.

Dear Former Volunteer:

By way of evaluating and improving our program we are asking that you take a minute and fill out the form below.

1. What was your position with ABC agency?_____
2. How long had you been involved?_____
3. How would you describe your feelings about your association with ABC agency?_____
4. Do you feel you received adequate training and supervision?_____
5. Do you feel it was a basically rewarding experience?_____
6. Did you have a comfortable relationship with co-workers?_____
   Staff?_____Comments:_____
7. Would you recommend to others that they become involved at ABC?___
8. Was your reason for leaving personal?_____ Did you have a conflict with scheduling?_____ Were you in some way dissatisfied with your experience?_____ Can you describe this?_____
9. Could you offer any suggestions for the improvement of volunteer activities and relationships at ABC agency?_____
10. Have you any additional comments which might be significant?_____

Thank You For Your Help!

The matter must not end here. The supervisor, director or Board president must be prepared to objectively consider the responses and to be willing to seek change for any factors that appear to be the cause of the dissatisfaction. After a few of these have been returned you will begin to get a picture of your program that profiles your strengths and weaknesses.

14. Publicity

"A 'Flexible Flyer' is More Than a Sled"

Most volunteer organizations at one time or another will want to share with the community news about their activities or to solicit help or financial support for their projects.

There are certain guidelines which the media will expect you to follow when seeking free coverage. They will vary somewhat from one station, magazine or paper to another, but there are basic considerations made by all.

Most local papers want material about interesting speakers or programs, charitable activities, awards presentations and elections, and to know if these are open to the public. Additionally, some papers will print feature articles with a human interest angle, such as three generations working to establish some worthy facility.

GETTING YOUR NEWS INTO THE MEDIA

What? Providing information about your group or organization offers access to the media. It puts your organization's name before the public in print, on television, or over the radio. It lets others know what you are doing or allows your spokesman's views to be quoted by a newspaper or in a television or radio broadcast.

Publicity may range from a brief mention in a round-up column, to a longer magazine feature; from a short announcement of a group activity on a radio broadcast, to an hour of air time.

How and Why? To generate news about your group or organization, you must have something newsworthy to offer. All media look for certain components that make a story appealing to their audience. These are: timeliness, importance to community, human interest and exclusive access to the information.

The media, especially newspapers, need information that they cannot always gather themselves. They depend on organizations for story ideas and news about their own events. Newsworthy stories help the media as well as provide publicity for you.

Several techniques can be used to generate publicity. The most basic is the news release. This is a story written in journalistic style and distributed to the appropriate media. News releases should have the most important information: who, what, when, where, why and how — in the first paragraph. Following paragraphs should provide more details, in descending order of importance.

In local newspapers, news releases are sometimes printed as is, or with minor editing. The lead paragraph may become the basis for a radio news story. News releases also provide background information to editors and new directors who assign reporters to develop a story.

Stories are also developed by local media from ideas suggested in letters, media alerts or telephone news tips. In all instances, it is essential that you provide information that the media consider newsworthy.

Story ideas have a better chance of receiving attention if they are directed to the proper editor, reporter or news director. Find out which reporter covers your organization and what he or she looks for in a story. The newspaper, television or radio station switchboard will usually give you the names of people to contact if you don't know them already.

When to Use. The timing of your publicity depends on the timeliness of your story. A quick-breaking news development can be relayed immediately by telephone. If you have an event planned, notify the media at least two weeks in advance. Talk show guests are usually booked eight weeks ahead.

Results. Publicity can provide valuable exposure and recognition of your organization. Offering positive stories to the media will help ensure that your side of the story is heard, even in negative situations, because you have established a dialogue with the media and are better understood by them.

Points to Remember:
- The media depend on information.
- Make sure your story is newsworthy.
- Put the most important elements in the first paragraph of a news release.
- Give the media ample notice of forthcoming events.

BASIC GUIDELINES FOR PUBLICITY

1. Begin all written material with your name, address and phone, and some identification on each succeeding sheet.
2. When providing background material remember: WHO, WHAT, WHERE, WHEN, WHY, and HOW.
3. Prepare your material with your audience in mind, and approach resources most likely to reach them.
4. Be newsworthy (timely, of importance, with prominent persons, in a special place, bringing about change, out of the ordinary, etc.).
5. Proof-read your work for accuracy of information, grammar and spelling.
6. For clarity or awkwardness of phrasing, re-read it with your reader in mind.

PRESS RELEASES

A press release is designed to let the media know of your planned project or event.
- Include all vital information.
- Send to news editors two weeks in advance (for daily and weekly publications).
- Your local media directory can give you deadlines and people to contact.
- Type your material on one side of 8½ x 11 paper.
- Indicate your preferred release date.
- Include a headline, presenting a summary of the story.

- Copy should be brief and concise, accurate and timely.
- Use first and last names and include identification, such as office held (do not include phone numbers).
- Always double space, and indent five spaces to begin a paragraph.
- Use 1¼ inch margins on all sides.
- Do not split a paragraph from one page to another.
- If more than one page is submitted, put "(more)" at the bottom of the page.
- Page numbers and identification should appear on each sheet.
- At the end, type "-30-", three lines relow the end of your copy.
- Send copies of good quality to each publication and maintain at least one for your files.
- Submit notices only if the event is open to the public.

SAMPLE NEWS RELEASE

Contact name
Street address
City, state, zip code
(area code) phone number
IDENTIFICATION LINE (slugline)　　　　　　　　RELEASE DATE
(such as <u>XYZ ORGANIZATION NATIONAL CONVENTION</u>)
Headline (all caps)
copy (double spaced, five spaces indent for paragraphs)
-30-

FACT SHEETS

A fact sheet presents information about your event in outline form. Use the same basic format as a Press Release. In this case complete sentences are not needed, and it is not necessary to use paragraph form.

- List five W's and "How" (or more specific words) in caps at the left — followed by a short answer
- Double space between elements
- Delete "more" and simply number additional sheets, if needed

SAMPLE FACT SHEET

Contact name
Street address
City, state, zip code
(area code) phone number
FACT SHEET ON (subject)   **Release Date**

WHAT: _____
FOR WHOM: _____
WHEN: _____
WHERE: _____
WHY: _____
HOW: _____
COST: _____
REGISTRATION: _____
SPEAKERS: _____
PROGRAMS: _____
SPONSORS: _____

-30-

TIP SHEETS

A "tip sheet" is used when inviting anyone from the media to come and cover your event. The form should briefly present WHO, WHAT, WHERE, WHEN and WHY. WHEN should be followed by the specific time and WHERE should include directions, if helpful.

PRESS KITS

A press kit is a collection of material distributed before a press conference or with an especially newsworthy press release. It is usually contained in a folder and includes:

- Cover letter
- Your news release
- A fact sheet
- Photo(s)
- Artist's renderings, if appropriate
- Background material on your organization
- Related material from an in-house magazine
- Your annual report, if appropriate

Only certain types of photos will generally be accepted by the media.

- Most often: taken by professional photographer and arranged for through the media
- When you submit: a 35 mm single-lens reflex produces the best photo
- 8½ x 10 black and white on glossy paper are preferred
- Polaroids are *not* acceptable
- Try to create an innovative setting without a distracting background
- Select subject matter relating to your story
- Try for a new angle; be original
- Crop to eliminate extraneous background material
- Provide sharp contrasts of light and dark
- Photos should be in perfect condition
- Include caption — brief and factual (which also states pertinent slug-line) and *contact* data, on the reverse side of the photo

PUBLIC SERVICE ANNOUNCEMENTS

Broadcasters are under no obligation to grant time to any group, nor is there any law that requires a station to devote a specific amount of time to community organizations. It has become a tradition among broadcasters to be sensitive to community needs and to communicate in the public interest.

Special programs are sometimes devoted to presentations, as are segments of regular programs. Also, there are:

SPOTS — Brief announcements made as time allows during the broadcast day

PERSONALITY SPOTS — Announcements made by recognizable personalities on behalf of a community project

NEW ITEMS — Short stories included in a regular newscast, briefly discussing a newsworthy event

EDITORIALS — Statements prepared which represent the station management's view on community programs or projects

Always telephone a station's Program Director for specific information regarding their public service policy. But before you do, become familiar with their programs so you know what you're talking about when you call.

Go prepared to any meeting with the Program Director. Know: WHAT the basic message is that you want to relay; WHO you want to reach (your audience); HOW you might best put across your message.

Remember, public service announcements are *only* available to non-profit organizations (and no time can be given to bingo or lotteries). Also, there will be many like you seeking free air time — and there is just so much of it.

You must obviously work in cooperation with the station and not expect any format changes or special arrangements. A taped or recorded announcement has the advantage of being available at numerous times, even if it isn't as appealing as a live interview, or as long.

Once you have made arrangements to meet with the Program Director, BE ON TIME, and go prepared. Written material for broadcasting falls into the same basic guidelines as that for print media. However, if a script is needed, be as informal as you would normally be in a speaking situation. For an interview provide a biographical sketch of the person to be interviewed, as well as six or eight points you hope to cover. (For difficult names — give phonetic spelling.)

To open the channels of communication, you might consider having a speaker from your local T.V. or radio station come to one of your meetings. This allows for great public relations. Your members will learn more about what the broadcasters do, and they will gain firsthand knowledge of your organization.

TIME ALLOTMENTS

	Radio time	T.V. time
10 seconds	25 words	20 words
20 seconds	50 words	40 words
30 seconds	75 words	60 words
60 seconds	150 words	125 words

For radio, be sufficiently descriptive so the listener can create a mental picture. For T.V., provide at least one slide or photograph for each ten seconds (and here, matte finished color slides are preferred). Request a return of your materials or they will be discarded. Film must be 16 mm *only*.

For radio, peripheral sounds can be very distracting, such as bracelets banging together. In T.V., softer colors are preferable to sharp contrasts, and you should not wear sparkling jewelry. Small prints and stripes do not transmit well and should be avoided.

It goes without saying, after any presentation or article has appeared, a note of appreciation should be sent.

The following is included as a form on which to outline local media contacts.

LOCAL MEDIA DATA

	NAME Newspapers, Magazines or Stations	CONTACT Editors, Columnists and Broadcasters	ADDRESS	PHONE
Newspapers:				
Magazines:				
Radio Stations:				
Television Stations:				

Reproduced courtesy of Rexnord Inc., Milwaukee, Wisconsin.

Other Organizations You Should Know About

American Broadcasting Company (ABC)
7 West 66 Street
New York, NY 10023
212/887-7777

Columbia Broadcasting System (CBS)
News Division
524 West 57th Street
New York, NY 10019
212/975-4114

National Broadcasting Company (NBC)
30 Rockefeller Plaza
New York, NY 10020
212/664-4444

Public Broadcasting Services (PBS)
475 L'Enfant Plaza West, SW
Washington, DC 20024
202/488-5000

Federal Communications Commission (FCC)
1919 M Street, NW
Washington, DC 20554
202/632-7000

National News Council
1 Lincoln Plaza
New York, NY 10023
212/595-944

National Public Radio (NPR)
2025 M Street, NW
Washington, DC 20036
202/822-2200

POSTERS

Posters can be an effective, inexpensive way to convey your message. They can be created for mass production by silk screening (do you have an artist in your group?), or can be made individually. In either case always create a rough draft first, to develop your concept, then sketch it on to your board in pencil.

For individual posters consider using wide felt markers or press type. Be sure to use letters large enough to be read easily from a distance. Graphics (art work of any kind) will greatly add to the eye appeal of your posters, as will key words like ATTENTION: SALE! NOTICE!

Your work should be done neatly and with care. Keep the lines straight and uniform. Bright colors have general appeal, but avoid gaudy shades and orange (which is hard to read from a distance). All pertinent information should appear and be easy to read. It should be laid out in an eye catching and memorable way.

Your next concern is for your audience. Where could you place the posters to reach those of most interest to you? schools? churches? shops? gas stations? (Be sure to obtain permission from the management before displaying any advertising material.)

FLYERS

Flyers require the same considerations as posters, except that they will be smaller in size and printed in bulk. The printing part implies that you must keep in mind the guidelines of photo-ready copy, such as preparing your original in black and white. It can be printed in eye-catching color.

Brevity, neatness and creativity will increase your chances of having it read.

The method of reproduction of your flyer will depend on your budget and how important it is that your material look professional. Mimeographed copies usually lack quality but may prove perfectly adequate for your needs.

Xerox copies can be quite expensive in the long run if you don't have access to a machine. Offset copies can be run more reasonably and give greater clarity. (Note: to test the ultimate effect of your draft and to see if it has all been laid out straight — make one xerox copy before ordering a volume of offset copies.) Laying out your material on half of a standard size sheet (such as 8½ x 11) will allow you to print twice as many without increasing the amount of paper stock.

DIRECT MAIL

Direct mail should be used only when you are certain of your audience and have access to an accurate mailing list. It is the most expensive approach because you must consider mailing costs in addition to printing.

Direct mail does have the advantage of reaching your audience directly and allowing the reader time to consider your information. If you are sending a letter, give it a personal touch. You could send along an informative fact sheet. Appearance is of the greatest importance. Type your letter on clear white paper with a carbon ribbon and place the material carefully on the page. Each copy should look like an original.

NEWSSHEETS

Before we consider the tools of the trade, I'd like to cover some common terms used in printing (see list in appendix). The first thing you'll be involved with is the *layout* of your *copy*. If you plan to type your material in preparation for the printer, it is important for you to know that reproductions made from *carbon ribbon* type will be of far better quality than those made from cloth ribbon type. Carbon ribbon produces cleaner, darker letters. Also, type on regular bond and correct with Liquid Paper, or correction tape.

Layout Techniques

If you are taking your material to a printer to *layout*, he will charge for this service and require a *dummy* — showing an idea of what the final product should look like on the pages. Learning to use graph paper and rubber cement will save you considerable money and could be a great challenge to your creativity. The graph paper is to assure that your typed lines appear straight and the rubber cement will allow you to move your copy if it isn't exactly right the first time (white glue will hold permanently). In lieu of a light table, hold your layout on the graph paper up to a light to check to see that lines appear straight.

In any case, you should begin by determining how much material you have and how much space it will take. After this you can create a "dummy" of paper folded to represent your final book. For example, one sheet folded becomes 4 pages: front, left middle, right middle and back. Each time you add a page, you really add 4. So when you fold a second sheet, you create an 8 page "dummy".

Having determined how much space your material will need, then decide visually in what manner to lay it out. You will discover that your graph paper will be numbered *out of order* for printing.

Taking an 8 page book, your graph sheets become:

Back	Cover	1	6	3	4	5	2

An article beginning on page 5 and continuing on page 6 will be laid out on separate graph sheets.

If you'd like to use fewer final sheets of paper (because printers charge by the sheet), consider laying out your material on graph paper 10⅔ x 13¾ and *reduce* the material by 25% for printing on 8½ x 11. Or, if it won't make the print too little, you could put it on 17 x 22 and reduce it 50% in the camera, to print on 8½ x 11.

This means each numbered page alone is 8½ x 11 on the graph paper. There will be a small charge for reduction, but a considerable savings in paper cost.

Always run the maximum number of copies at one time — prices go down by volume. Also, there are basic charges which will be repeated each time you reprint. Two-sided printing is only 90% more expensive than a one-sided sheet. (Two one-sided sheets will cost more.)

When doing your own final layout you can create bold headlines by purchasing press type (rub on) letters or clip art at stationery, college bookstores, and art supply stores. Using your graph paper, these letters can be pressed on graph paper to spell out the needed headings. (Be sure to follow the directions in the package.)

To add to the eye appeal of your newssheet, black and white line drawings and borders may be clipped from good quality magazines (such as The New Yorker). Avoid clutter and for ideas about effective placement, look at other magazines. Be sure to leave enough "white space" to create a balanced effect and a half inch of "grab space" for the machine to grip your material at the top, or bottom, during printing.

Using a pale blue pencil you can make guidelines or even notes to your printer, as this will not reproduce. Red will reproduce as black, but blue will not reproduce at all, which is why graph paper is printed in blue.

Printing

When you are ready to take your material to the printer go fully prepared, have all the information decided about size, color, paper and quantity. He will not want the burden of these decisions. They must be yours. AND, your material must be thoroughly proofed; it is not part of his job to catch *your* errors.

Prepare your material well in advance of your needed deadline, to allow for the printer's schedule. You might consider contracting with the printer to save a certain day each month for your printing job, but be sure to keep your part of the bargain. If you plan to mail your materials, remember that Uncle Sam's post office needs time to play its tricks.

PRACTICAL POINTS TO PONDER ABOUT PHOTO-READY COPY

1. Typing should be done with CARBON RIBBON on clean white regular bond paper with an electric typewriter.
2. Corrections should be made with SNOPAKE (liquid paper) or correction tape; do not use onion paper and erase.
3. Margin notes may be made to the printer in pale blue pencil; this does not photograph.
4. Captions, borders, pictures and such should be secured in place with rubber cement; this allows for changes.

5. Cartoons, borders and captions can be clipped from sources such as *New Yorker* and *Phoenix* magazine (or others printed on glossy paper), and reproduced directly, with permission.

6. Clip-art books are available with borders and art work for use without permission.

7. Art and college bookstores sell transfer and press type letters for use in captions (without the expense of type setting).

8. Photographs should be in black and white — and require additional time for the printer to *screen* them or to prepare metal plates for good reproduction.

9. Red reproduces as black, and most other colors as shades of gray.

10. In the end, you are ultimately responsible for any errors; not the printer! Proofread before and after copy goes to the typist.

11. Anticipate in advance as many of your needs as possible to avoid delays and to save on costs. Several pictures can be screened at one time and later printed separately. All covers can be printed in color at one time, and only one color change fee will be required.

12. When possible to arrange, do all layouts on a light table or following pale blue lines (such as graph paper) ... to assure accuracy. Enlargements and reductions will add to your cost.

13. There are machines that: staple, collate, saddle stitch (staple in a fold), drill holes, fold (in numerous ways).

14. Colored ink, heavy or unusual paper and photographs all add to routine printing costs, as does layout if your material isn't photo ready.

15. When printing on two sides, time must be allowed for the first side to dry prior to printing the reverse. This is also the case before collating, folding and drilling.

16. Enlargements and reductions will add to your cost, but may be done in advance of printing by having your original reduced on a large copier capable of the process.

15. Career Development

"From the House to the Senate"

The main point I want to make in this chapter is simply that you can do just about anything you set your mind to do. But it takes planning. It is unreasonable to presume, just because you were always good in math, that you can be the financial advisor to a large corporation next week.

That isn't to say you can *never* be the financial advisor, only that you must take specific steps to get there. You could become involved, through volunteer work, as the treasurer of an organization or chairman of major fund raisers, and begin to make contacts; finally, by determining and seeking the necessary course work, perhaps as a part-time college student.

Have you developed marketable skills such as advertising, selling ads for your news magazine or program? Or done graphic work, such as layouts for either of the above? Perhaps you have been a conference coordinator or tour guide. Have you administered a large project or initiated a new program?

MAKE IT HAPPEN

Begin to look at what you have done in terms of achievements and specific knowledge and open up your thinking to consider where, in the world of employment, there might be a market for these skills. Then develop a marketing plan — to sell yourself to a specific employer.

Don't rely on an employment agency to find something for you, or to come upon that great *find* in the want ads. You'll have to *make it happen;* you must take charge. It's your life; it should be your choice.

It is possible to parlay your skills, experience and understanding of a volunteer activity into a staff position with that organization. Submit an application, if and when an opening develops. Chances are you already have a track record and friends to speak on your behalf. Most of these positions go to people agencies know about.

It is my feeling that any assertive, dependable person, with leadership experience in the volunteer segment, possesses the skills needed to do any non-technical administrative job and supervise others.

Most social service organizations have some paid staff, and at any one time, one will be looking for a person with the very kind of skills most volunteer leaders have acquired. Look in the Yellow Pages, drop by your local Volunteer Bureau or Voluntary Action Center. Of the agencies listed, which sound most interesting to you? Research them, fully — then develop a sales pitch designed to sell yourself to the organization of your choosing. Tell them why they can't live without you!

You may not have the needed college degree or work background, but I'll bet you have the "Equivalent Experience." This is true not only in specific social service agencies — but with groups such as professional fund-raisers.

Once you secure just one paid position you put yourself into a different category when it comes to looking for work. You have a recent successful experience doing something many find immediately more credible.

Shirley Fader, in *From Kitchen to Career*, recommends that you look at your pre-marriage occupation and add your volunteer work to the picture. What you have is a new mix of talent, training and experience which can be parlayed into a lucrative position, if you are willing to make it happen.

This requires a bit of creative thinking, such as suggested above. You may have an insight no one else has and can create a job previously non-existent. Recognize that you do have valuable expertise and market it! Convince potential employers that they need you. Be specific about what you can do for them and document your experience. (See form at end of Chapter).

THE IDEAL JOB

What would your ideal job look like? Can you describe it? What kind of activity interests you?

- How many hours a week do you want to work?
- In what kind of setting?

- Would you prefer working with tasks, or people?
- Do you want to work on your own with a flexible schedule in a workplace?
- Do you want structure and guidance or freedom to be creative and responsible for your own time?
- What sort of people would you find interesting as co-workers, as supervisors, as recipients of your service?
- What skills and talents would you like challenged?
- What *kinds* of things do you have experience with and what would you like to work with (cameras, food, computers, phones, numbers, paper, etc.)?

If economics will allow you the luxury, initially you can consider entering the field of your choice by offering to work on a specific project (administrating, fund raising, ad selling) to prove yourself, before acquiring employment status. Remember, up to this point you have been working on a voluntary basis anyway! You might ask for a fee figured as a percentage of ads solicited or funds raised, or after a program has been deemed successful.

Whether you are looking for your first real job or returning to work after years away from your field, securing a position ultimately depends on how prepared you are to discuss a specific opening and how *you* could best fill it, how articulate you are, how much self-assurance you radiate, and how positive you appear. This all comes out in the job interview.

TARGET MARKETING YOURSELF

▲ Figure out what you can do best and where you could do it (see Self Assessment).
▲ Present yourself to the employer of your choice (even if he doesn't know yet that he needs you!)
▲ Go prepared to a job search with a resumé — an adertisement which promotes you.
▲ Develop a complete marketing plan — where *you* are the product.

I. Resumé

Do:
- Prepare a cover letter indicating briefly what is enclosed and why it is of importance to the potential employer. Sign boldly and legibly.

- Keep resumé in outline form where possible; otherwise, very short sentences.
- Use strong verbs and active voice ("Directed $50,000 Fund Raiser" — rather than "was appointed chairman of the Rummage Sale").
- List achievements on a second sheet in descending order of importance.
- Follow itemized list with functional list, to better convince the employer that your volunteer skills are transferable.
- Have your resumés photo-copied or professionally printed to make each look like a clear original.

Don't:
- Don't use a resumé service to write your resumé; you might become too much of someone else's packaged product.
- Don't be cute — no pink paper or artsy typeface, oversize paper, catchy borders. Prepare a professional looking form.
- Don't mention why you left your last job (if you had one).
- Don't abuse your friendships by expecting too much from those you ask to serve as references. Keep references to a minimum and of an impressive nature. On your resumé you might state: References upon request.
- Don't quote a salary figure or mention a previous one (even if you have received one).
- Don't adapt someone else's resumé; work from a guide such as the one in this chapter.
- Don't lie or purposely mislead.
- Don't editorialize or talk in the third person.

II. The Interview

1. Points to remember before going for an interview:
   - When you don't really care if you get the job or not, go through a dry run or a low-stress interview with a friend.
   - If possible schedule your appointment before lunch, early in the week.
2. Remember that the command of the situation belongs with the interviewer. However:
   - Arrive early, dressed for the job (no perfume or unnecessary jewelry).
   - Consider carrying a good-looking briefcase (if it suits the job you seek).

- Be cordial and pleasant.
- Shake hands firmly and look directly into the eye of the interviewer when you introduce yourself.
- Sit in a chair close to the desk, sit tall and lean toward the interviewer (this implies interest and attentiveness).

3. Limit your interviews to companies you feel truly qualified to work for in some *specific* capacity.
    - Do a thorough self assesment first.
    - Be enthusiastic about what you have done and what you feel you could bring to the prospective position.
    - Be positive and truthful.
    - Project attentiveness and ask for clarification of anything you don't understand.
    - Show that you believe in yourself without tooting your own horn or belittling yourself.
    - Project self-respect and make it clear you won't compromise yourself just to get a job.
    - Never criticize a former employer.
    - Don't ever accept a salary offer at the initial interview (if they really want you, you'll find you have a little leverage; don't underestimate yourself).
    - Always follow up an interview with a thank-you note.

4. When it appears you will not get a position:
    - Learn what specific drawbacks you have.
    - Ask about what was seen as your strong point.
    - Remember another position might open at another time. Keep your impression a good one.
    - Don't become discouraged — it probably simply means that someone else was more qualified for the job at this time or that his presentation was better.

III. Traps in the Interview

To best prepare yourself for these, consider some of the questions you're apt to face ... and what the interviewer *really* wants to know:

- "Tell me about yourself"
  (Are you flexible, cooperative, liked by co-workers?)
- "Which of your jobs did you enjoy most?"
  (Will our position be right for you — will you thrive in this environment?)

- "How old are you?"
  (Are you reliable? They aren't considering age per se, but maturity and independence and responsibility.)
- "Can you travel or work overtime?"
  (Do you have family responsibilities which will interfere with your job?)
- "Tell me about your hobbies."
  (How much of your personal time or contacts may help us?)
- "What do you consider one of your weaknesses?"
  (In other words, can you accept constructive criticism? Show them you are capable of a realistic appraisal of your feelings and are interested in overcoming any weaknesses.)
- "What are your future plans?"
  (Beware. They want to determine how long you expect to be with their company.)

Generally speaking, a potential employer will not be interested in looking through your every certificate or award. But documenting your volunteer experiences could be the first step in developing a career portfolio. A complete record of your involvement will enable you to analyze the functions you can perform and the skills you have acquired.

Whenever possible avoid the personnel department. Determine the type of work you feel qualified to handle and seek out the individual who would become your supervisor . . . then *sell yourself*.

The following may help you to determine your areas of expertise and help you plan for your future. With the information revealed, you can determine which new skills you may want to acquire, and what direction you want to take. (Employment applications are now being redesigned to list questions and provide space for information about volunteer experience.)

SAMPLING OF DOCUMENTATION

- Resumé
- Job descriptions
- Letters of commendation
- Citations/awards/certificates
- News clippings
- Samples of your work:
     displays/exhibits
     posters
     press releases

flyers
brochures
workshops developed
proposals written
photographs taken
slide shows developed
manuals prepared
charts/graphs/maps

- Audio or visual tapes of you in action:
  speaking
  training
  counseling
  interviewing
  demonstrating
- Letters of recommendation from:
  agency executives
  local leaders
  city planners

Volunteer opportunities provide on-the-job training, a chance at an internship, as well as an opportunity to determine, at little risk, whether a position in this field or that would be truly satisfying. Teenagers, especially, who face the obstacle of "EXPERIENCE NEEDED" can profit from volunteer involvement. Time invested in a volunteer position not only provides documented experience but many times it opens doors by providing contacts for paid positions.

To realistically plan for a career, and to use your volunteer activity as a springboard, you might review the section on Self Assessment. Without a clear picture of who you are and what you can do, it is difficult to develop a reasonable plan about where you might go and how you might get there.

Focus on your *achievements* (those activities which gave you a feeling of pride), rather than merely your *accomplishments* (which are things you simply did). Concentrating on these activities will help you to get a better idea of what you derive satisfaction from doing, and thus what would bring you pleasure in the working world.

CREDIT FOR VOLUNTEER SKILLS

During the 60's a national task force of educators developed a tool called The Continuing Education Unit (C.E.U.) This unit represents ten contact hours of participation in an organized, continuing education experience under responsible sponsorship, capable direction and qualified instruction. These C.E.U.'s carry no academic credit, nor are they accompanied by grades. The type of training they catalog is considered "post secondary". Many community colleges are awarding C.E.U.'s for their non-credit courses. These units quantify and validate training.

Accreditation is a process of peer review that results in public accountability — the approval by contemporary associates of the process, method, content and ethics of a course.

If you are transferring volunteer experience to a U.S. Civil Service job, you will find C.E.U.'s recognized in determining entry to mid-level technical and professional jobs.

FUNCTIONAL RESUMÉ GUIDELINE**
(Suggestions)

Vicki Volunteer   Date
Address
City, State, Zip Code
Phone

FAMILY:

EDUCATION:
    (Include degrees and honors)

OBJECTIVE (position sought):

EMPLOYMENT EXPERIENCE:

VOLUNTEER EXPERIENCE:
    (Use when and where applicable)

    ▲Administrative-
       Organized. . .
       Coordinated. . .
       Implemented. . .
       Designed. . .
       Initiated. . .
       Supervised. . .
       Directed. . .
       Activated. . .

    ▲Parliamentary Law/By-laws Interpretation-
       Put together. . .
       Interpreted. . .

Acted as. . .
Translated. . .
Appointed to. . .

▲Education/Public Speaking-
Compiled. . .
Debated. . .
Addressed. . .
Spoke to. . .
Moderated. . .

▲Advocacy-
Evaluated. . .
Advocated for. . .
Presented. . .
Provided. . .

▲Financial Management/Budgeting-
Reviewed. . .
Studied. . .
Developed. . .
Participated in. . .
Assisted in. . .
Executed. . .

▲Leadership-
Elected. . .
Acted as. . .
Administered. . .
Presided over. . .
Proposed. . .
Executed. . .

▲Project Development-
Originated. . .
Planned. . .
Delegated. . .
Participated in. . .
Advocated for. . .

▲Communication-
Wrote. . .
Edited. . .
Drafted. . .
Summarized. . .
Interpreted. . .

▲Research-
   Designed. . .
   Drafted. . .
   Reviewed. . .
   Researched. . .
   Developed. . .

▲Training-
   Workshop experience in. . .
   Seminars attended. . .
   Conferences participated in. . .
   Conventions attended. . .
   Independent course work. . .
   Skills I can teach. . .

REFERENCES:
   (Organization presidents, volunteer directors, principals, etc.)

CONCLUSION:
   Conclude with your perception of the qualifications needed for the position you are seeking and how you feel your background has prepared you to succeed in such a position.

(**Based on a resumé drawn up by Joan Smith for an area position with the Association of Junior Leagues)

APPENDIX

"and in conclusion. . ."

The material included in the appendix seemed appropriate for a book on Skills for Leadership, but somehow did not fit into any particular chapter. For this reason I have chosen to include these selections at the end. In each case, as with the material in the preceding chapters, these tools will only be helpful if you put them to use! Adapt, edit, revise, but use the enclosed material.

RESEARCH AND INTERVIEWING
Based on material by Susan Shultz, columnist, editor and executive search consultant (used with permission)

KEY ELEMENTS:

I. Types of Interviews:
  A. Acquiring Information (Seeking feedback, exploring issues, gathering data)
  B. Giving Information (Sharing information, as in chairing a committee)
  C. Advocating (Modifying beliefs or attitudes, as in lobbying)

D. Problem Solving (Resolving conflict or seeking solutions)

II. Preparation:

A. Research — the more you know before you go in, the more you are likely to know coming out

B. Let your interviewee know specifically what you are seeking, so he can be prepared

C. Establish your Goals and Objectives for the session, in advance

D. Outline your questions ahead of time, but don't be inflexible (Listen, be responsive, watch carefully and be prepared to modify your approach)

III. Before the Interview:

A. Define the information Objectives

B. Determine WHOM you will interview

C. Writing your questions -

1. Avoid ambiguous wording or biased direction

2. Keep questions conversational, simple, and short

3. Avoid questions with two elements

4. Avoid loaded, biased questions

5. Consider the effects of one question on another

D. Pre-test your questions, when possible

E. Contacting the Interviewee -

1. Precede your interview with a letter or phone call indicating the range of questions, and time needed

2. If your interview is related to your organization, include a brochure and be prepared to answer questions about it

IV. Creating the Atmosphere:

A. Go fully prepared, knowing what you need to know

B. Establish a rapport. Make it easy for the interviewee to talk to you

C. Your job is primarily one of reporter — take all opinions in your stride without surprise or disapproval

D. Maintain control over the direction of the interview

E. Be aware of your own biases and don't let them interfere

F. Listen — Let your respondent know you care about what he has to say

V. Types of Interview Questions:

  A. *Low Structured Questions* - call for a specific response of a few words (Often begin with *Have, Are, Did, Will, Do*).

  B. *High Structured Questions* - Open-ended, designed to evoke more than enumerations or hard, concise facts. (Usually begin *Like, How, What, Why, Tell*).

  C. *Mirroring Questions* - Parroting to gain elaboration, non-judgmental (Usually a re-statement to keep the focus on the respondent).

  D. *Probe Questions** - Bridging questions, to probe for more depth (Short statement such as "Why?", "How is that?", designed to keep him talking).

  E. *Leading Questions* - Strongly imply or encourage a specific answer. To confirm suspicions or test someone (Can be produced by words, tone of voice or expressions of bias).

  F. *Clarifying Questions* - Closure questions at the end to summarize; to insure that you understand what the respondent has said. ("Let me rephrase that. ...", "As I understand it. ..", "What you are saying is. ..").

VI. Recording and Reporting:

  A. Check your notes for accuracy and thoroughness. Make corrections immediately.

  B. Reporting verbatim responses indicates attitudes, maintaining meaning as well as emphasis

  C. Separate fact from opinion and your reactions in the written report. Draw up your final report while your information is fresh

  D. Record:

    1. As the interview progresses

    2. For accuracy, read back information of which you are unsure

    3. If appropriate, send a letter with a rebuttal proviso, summarizing any positions taken or commitments made

    4. Always clarify the use to which the interview will be put

The process is not finished until you have sent off a note of thanks to the individual sharing his time and knowledge with you.

Always date your material, identify yourself as the author, and make a copy for yourself before sending off your report.

*When To Probe

  If the response is:

  1. *Inadequate, irrelevant or too vague*

  2. *Contradictory, or an avoidance of the question*

  3. *Limited, incomplete, non-specific*

REFERENCE FORM
VOLUNTEER WORK EXPERIENCE

Volunteer:

    Name:_____

    Address:_____

    Phone:_____

Organization or Agency served:

    Name:_____

    Address:_____

    Phone:_____

    Supervisor:_____

Volunteer Job Title:_____

Describe skills, knowledge and abilities used to perform duties and responsibilities of the job (include tools and equipment used):

_____

_____

_____

_____

Dates of service in this volunteer position: from: _____ to: _____

Actual hours served in this job: _____ per day   _____ per week

                                        _____ per month _____ total hours

Reason for leaving this position:_____

Signature of Director of Volunteers or Supervisors:

_____ Date: _____

    Name:_____

    Title:_____

    Address:_____

    Phone:_____

(Volunteer: Retain this form for your record, it is a certification of your volunteer work experience and may be used as a job reference.)

GUIDELINE FOR PROPOSALS

Clearly state:
- Your over-all goal
- Your subsequent objectives
- Specifically what you propose to accomplish
- Why this is a significant goal and these are important objectives
- How you propose to accomplish this

Project your resource expenditure:
- How you will staff it (do it)?
- What is the suggested time schedule for preparation and for the event itself?
- What will be the line of authority and responsibility?
- What resources do you have, (such as money and material)?
- What additional resources will you need?

What evidence is there that such a program or project will be successful?

How do you plan to evaluate the results?

If your proposal is to go to a major corporation or government agency, professional help is worth considering. Investing a relatively small sum in a consultant, may produce great rewards in terms of a grant or corporation funding.

Proposals often are turned down because of inadequacies in preparation. Below are five reasons most often given:

1. Insufficient evidence is given that the project can sustain itself beyond the life of the funding or grant.
2. The goals and objectives have not been clearly stated, nor is it clear how it is to be implemented.
3. The objectives do not coincide with those of the funding source.
4. The monetary requirements of the project cannot be met by the agency approached.
5. Finally, and simply, the proposal is poorly written and hard to understand.

Always present the agency a clear, neat, typed copy well in advance of your deadline. It should be double spaced with wide margins. When binding, whether in a folder or notebook, take care to protect the pages, include pertinent supplementary material, a cover sheet, and a note as to who your contact person is.

If you are working on a smaller scale, the same general guidelines apply. Your final product may appear as a single sheet, such as a proposal for a fundraiser prepared for consideration by your Board or general membership, but it should still spell out each of the key points listed.

My purpose for including this material is to help you in communicating your hopes to those in a position to approve or veto your ideas. If you are concerned more specifically with major funding and fund-raising projects per se, I refer you to Suggested Reading.

PROGRAM ADVERTISING

Beyond the profits of the door receipts, from any baseball tournament, cabaret or variety show, your Program is a great source of potential revenue. Here are some suggestions on how to approach Program advertising:

1. Start with friends of friends. Ask your members to list as many individuals and their firms as possible. This will give you a more personalized "in". From here you can then:

   a. Ask each to call or write to their contacts and to individually promote your cause. (They will obviously require a Fact sheet, and guidelines regarding the specific requirements about such things as payment and photo-ready material) or

   b. You can compile a cross reference list and assign a committee to prepare letters with a personal touch (i.e. "John Jones was sure you would want to place an ad in our program.") Itemize the specifics of the purchase of the ad as well as who your market will be and how many you expect to reach.

2. Second, in either case, is to send a follow-up letter with the specifics of your proposal in writing. There are special typewriters than can be programmed to personalize each letter ("word processors") — such services should be sought as a *donation*, with a tax write-off to the firm.

3. Within two weeks a follow-up phone call should be made to offer to consider any questions (obviously to give an additional sales pitch) and to make arrangements for getting the layout material to be used ("photo-ready" greatly simplifies things).

4. Stay away from the individuals in every firm programmed to say no. Try by phone, when you have no "in", to determine who the best person is to talk to, and address your letters to him. Also determine when they set up their budget and how early you need to approach them.

5. Beyond this, it is possible to go directly to a local advertising firm in your community known to handle the companies that you are interested in attracting. They can make arrangements for you but will charge a percentage.

6. Charge what the market will bear, but remember your audience. Different events appeal to different individuals and thus become appealing to different advertisers. Some are more accustomed than others to paying steep prices for advertising.

7. Consider sponsorships which allow the advertiser to have his product at your event, or to merchandise in some way in conjunction with the event. (Also, some firms will not buy an ad unless they will be exclusive — such as no other pop brand).

8. Once you are ready to prepare the final draft of your program, check around for volunteer assistance. Printing from Photo-ready copy can save you thousands of dollars in "Layout fees" (see the section on newssheet production for guidelines).

HOW TO DESIGN A QUESTIONNAIRE

Determine First:
- What information is wanted
- The type of questions to use

Then:
- The content of each question
- The wording of the question
- The sequence of the questions

Finally:
- Design the layout and reproduction
- Pre-test the questionnaire
- And *THEN* revise and draft the final questionnaire

Considerations:
1. Content
   - Is the question really needed at all?
   - Are several questions needed instead of one?
   - Can the respondent be expected to be knowledgable or is he opinionated?
   - Can the respondent be expected to answer the question (is he able to phrase and answer in writing, to share his information?)
2. Type of Questions
   - Multiple choice — often none of the choices given really fits; on the other hand, this approach may help the respondent focus. These are easy to tabulate.
   - Dichotomous — two extremes such as "yes" or "no"
   - Open ended — this technique gives the respondent a chance to answer in his own words and is often more revealing (useful as a first question)
   - Scaled — such as a 1 to 10 rating
   - Ranking — listing preferred choices in order
3. Wording
   - Remember the journalists' five w's: who, what, where, when and why. Occasionally "how" is also pertinent.
   - Avoid questions that may appear unreasonable from the respondent's perspective.
   - Never use "leading" questions. You will only hear what you want to hear and the question becomes negated.
   - Use simple words. Each word should have only one meaning.
   - Steer away from ambiguous words that can be interpreted differently by different people (i.e. "frequently", "normally", "occasionally", etc.)

4. Sequence
   - The first question should always be designed to pique the interest of the respondent.
   - Consider the influence one question may have on another. Where possible, ask questions after the fact, so as not to bias the responses to the other question.
   - Hide difficult questions in the middle or end. As the respondent becomes involved in the process of answering, these should become easier to answer.
   - Follow a logical order. Think in terms of the respondent's viewpoint, where possible.

TIDBITS FROM TRAINING

1. Always date and identify any material you prepare.
2. Always keep at least one copy, or the original, of any material you entrust to the U.S. mails.
3. We may all be looking at the same thing, but we're each seeing things differently.
4. You get out of life what you put into it.
5. Personal identity and fulfillment come from serving others.
6. Always have a Plan B.
7. Get to know yourself. Do what you enjoy most and do best.
8. Look for the positive; deal graciously with the negative.
9. If you don't plan to do it in the best way possible, don't say you'll do it.
10. Conflict should be resolved, not avoided.
11. We remember only 30 percent of what we see and 20 percent of what we hear.
12. Advanced planning pays off in time saved in the end.
13. Consider other people's needs.
14. To find productive solutions, your group should feel like a team with a common goal.
15. Never call a meeting just to call a meeting.
16. State your expectations clearly, in the beginning.
17. If you don't manage your own time, someone less qualified will do it for you.
18. Agendas should be specific — time frames, topics and individual responsibilities spelled out.
19. Decisions are no better than the information on which they are based.
20. To evaluate is not to criticize, but to consider critically.
21. Select the best time of day to tackle each task.
22. If you do not do it right the first time, when will you have time to do it over?
23. Use blank spaces in your day.
24. When bogged down, move on to another project.
25. "A person's self-esteem is his most important commodity." (Charles Hobbs)
26. Make decisions at the lowest level possible.
27. Take solutions, not problems, to the authority.
28. Set realistic deadlines for yourself and others.
29. Precede criticism with two words of praise.
30. Surround and identify yourself with successful people.

STEPS IN MAKING A PRESENTATION

I. Five Elements of a Presentation
   A. Pre-presentation
   B. The Beginning
   C. The Body
   D. The End
   E. Post-presentation analysis

II. Pre-presentation
   A. Examine the five W's
      1. *Who?* May include:
         a. Presenters — trainers or facilitators
         b. Participants — all those who will be receiving the presentation
         c. Others — anyone else whose views or input will influence the presentation
      2. *What?* The subject to be covered in the presentation
      3. *Why?* Clearly define objectives for the session
      4. *Where?* Location (all environmental factors should be examined)
      5. *When?* Date and time
   B. Planning — begins with analysis of the answers to the five W's
      1. Have reasonable objectives been set?
      2. What background and experience will audience be bringing to the presentation?
      3. What do they expect from the session?
      4. What is the scope and depth of the material to be covered?
      5. What resources are available to be used for the presentation?
      6. What background and ability are you, the presenter, bringing to the session?
      7. What limitations are involved? (time, space, etc.)
   C. Formalizing — develop the specifics of the plan
      1. Do you have an agenda and workable time frame?
      2. Have you defined participant activities and responsibilities, if there are any?
      3. Have you decided on specific as well as general methods to use?
   D. Preparing — take care of the details
      1. Have you completed all handouts, guides, references, etc.?
      2. Have you confirmed all coordinating elements?
      3. Have you practiced with equipment — A.V. (Audio visuals), public address systems, etc.?
      4. Have you held a critiqued rehearsal to evaluate both content and delivery?
      5. Have your arrived early enough to check and/or adjust any on-site preparation?

III. The Beginning
   A. The presenter has four minutes to set the mood!
      1. You must command audience attention, beyond the introduction you've been given.
      2. Choose a method that is comfortable for you and appropriate to the situation
   B. Pay attention to style
      1. Notes — what kind are best for you? (3 x 5 cards, 'ghost writing')
      2. Eliminate barriers such as podiums
      3. Gear your vocabulary to the group, but don't talk down
      4. Watch your mannerisms
   C. Establish the fundamentals of the presentation
      1. State the objectives, for approval
      2. Establish any other conditions or ground rules (norms)
      3. Relate presentation to any preceding or subsequent presentations
   D. Stimulate the participants to activity (must be done early in the session)

IV. The Body
   A. Fundamental methods
      1. Telling or lecturing
         a. Inductive vs. deductive approach
         b. Whole-part-whole method
         c. Effective use of questions
      2. Showing or demonstrating
         a. Requires careful planning
         b. Alternatives should be available
      3. Participating
         a. *Brainstorming* — controlled process to stimulate creativity
         b. *Discussion* — presenter should maintain role as facilitator and not inflict opinions
         c. *Buzz Groups* — discussion groups in which number of participants equals time spent (6 x 6 or 6 people discussing for 6 minutes). Can be used to reach consensus
         d. *Case Study* — an actual hypothetical situation which is particularly useful in problem solving
         e. *Role Playing* — participants act out a given situation which may or may not have a built-in conclusion
         f. *Dyads, Tryads* — groups of 2 or 3 people who perform a task. Particularly effective in practicing communication and listening skills
         g. *Exercises* — any structured activity which relates to the presentation

B. Feedback — throughout the presentation the feedback system must work at full efficiency
   1. Both verbal and non-verbal reactions should be received and analyzed
      a. Watch the process
      b. Use clarifying techniques — "What I hear you saying ..." "Do I understand you to mean ..."
   2. Be aware of any environmental factors which are influencing the presentation (temperature, light, noise, smoke, etc.)
   3. Make spontaneous adjustments — be flexible in either technique or environment, if necessary

V. The Ending
   A. Should be planned and prepared but may be adjusted to reflect feedback
      1. Summarize
      2. Relate parts to the whole
      3. Re-inforce key points but don't be redundant
   B. Conduct an evaluation — written, verbal or both

VI. Post-presentation analysis
   A. Were the objectives met?
      1. What factors contributed to success? Build these into future presentations (*P*reserve)
      2. What factors could be improved upon (*I*mprove)
      3. What factors detracted? Negate or neutralize these (*E*liminate)
   B. Revise and refine the presentation
   C. Begin pre-presentation phase of next presentation

PRINTING TERMS

BANNER — Bold headline beginning a printed sheet, usually full width of the page

BLEED — a term used to refer to the image extending to the edge of the page

BLIND EMBOSSED — a design stamped into the page/texture without ink

BLOW-UP — an enlargement

BOLD FACE TYPE — headline, heavier type

CAMERA-READY (photo-ready) — EXACT representation of material as you want it to appear (may be enlarged or reduced)

COLLATE — to assemble pages in order

COPY — written material; the articles or message

CROP — to cut off a portion, usually unneeded material in a photograph

CUT — a photo engraving

CUTLINE — text to go with an illustration

DECKLE EDGE — untrimmed feather edge of paper

DUMMY — mock-up of a proposed publication with all the components of the final product

ELEMENT — a changeable type ball (each contains a distinct type style) for use on various electric typewriters

ELITE — providing 12 characters to the linear inch, 6 lines to the vertical inch

ENLARGEMENT — a copy made larger than the original

FILLER — optional material to be used when articles run short

FOLD — to crease and turn down at one or more locations on the page — must be done after the ink has had time to dry

FORMAT — basic design, giving size, shape and sequence of a proposed composition

GLOSSY — a photograph printed on shiny paper

GRIPPER SPACE — ½ inch needed on the lead edge of the paper where it is grabbed and pulled through the press. No copy can appear here.

GUTTER — the blank space, or inner margin, from the printing area to the binding

HALF TONE (PMT) — a photograph converted to a dot pattern — made by photographing a picture through a screen — essential for offset reproduction

INSERT — an extra section or page inserted loosely after binding

JUSTIFY — to space out lines uniformly to the same length

LAYOUT — a diagram showing what the printed product should look like; the placement of items on the page

LEAD — first paragraph of a news release

LITHOGRAPHY — printing method involving a chemical or photographic process, based on the principle that oil and water don't mix

LOGO — a product or company trademark

LOWER CASE — small letters in type — not capitals

MECHANICAL BINDING — holes are punched and plastic or metal coils inserted

MEDIA — channels of communication

NEWSPRINT — cheap quality paper usually used for newspapers

OFFSET — see LITHOGRAPHY

OPAQUE — paper of a less than transparent nature

PASTE-UP — the prepared copy for the printer — layout in final form

PICA — unit of type — 1/16 inch or 12 point.

POSITIVE — the reverse of a negative

REAM — 500 sheets of paper

REDUCTION — a print made smaller than the original

REGISTER — fitting two or more printing images in exact alignment

ROUGH — a preliminary draft of a proposed layout

RUN — number of copies to be printed at one time

SCREEN — to convert a photo to half tones

SETOFF — ink from one sheet leaving a mark on a neighboring sheet

SADDLE STITCH — staple in the middle of a folded page

TRANSFER TYPE — type available on plastic sheets and applied to a page by rubbing the letters onto a page (press type), or clipping out and securing

TYPE FACE — the name given to a design of type

UPPER CASE — all capital letters

WHITE SPACE — space left without copy or pictures, to create a clean, uncluttered appearance

PAPER TERMS

COATED STOCK — a non-porous offset paper, available in matte or glossy finish, normally heavier than bond

COVER STOCK — heavier paper used to cover catalogs and such

GRAIN — the direction of the grain in a sheet of paper (paper folds and tears more easily *with* the grain)

BULK — the thickness of the paper (bulkier paper will make a short report appear longer)

WEIGHT — this is figured in pounds of 500 sheets of *standard size paper* — these standard sizes vary for each type of paper

OPACITY — the capability of paper to take ink on one side without its showing through on the other side — the heavier and bulkier the paper, the more opaque it is

COLOR — this element is important because color conveys a message and the one you choose should be appropriate to the intended message

FINISH — the way in which the surface of the paper has been treated — certain images reproduce better on one kind of paper, such as half tones on coated stock

LIABILITIES

Any time an organization incorporates, it enters a new category in terms of liability. It is important that Articles of Incorporation contain provisions for mandatory indemnification of Board members.

Your name on a letterhead can place you in liability. Insurance against officer and director liability is, unfortunately, a must. Provisions should be made in your Bylaws for the automatic removal of a director who does not participate or who behaves in a manner inconsistent with the policies of the Board.

A non-profit organization takes on the same powers as other corporations, which implies it can contract, sue, be sued, own property and continue to exist independent of any one person. It has a separate legal identity and its liability is limited to the corporation's assets.

The non-profit corporation must be governed by a Board of Directors, with fiduciary responsibility. These Directors must answer to the corporation, its members, and the state attorney general. This includes compliance with all IRS and other federal and state requirements. Directors may be held accountable even for acts committed in ignorance of the law.

Special care should be taken when accepting federal and state grant money. Government rules are easy to overlook and misunderstand. Miscalculations can be costly. Here it is especially important to have qualified legal counsel. If a corporation cannot account for grant funds it receives, each board member may be held liable for the full amount! Accepting any grant money means entering into a contractual obligation.

One of the best ways to minimize risks is to have an annual audit by a certified public accountant. ("Certified" because they carry malpractice insurance). It is a responsibiity of the Board to select a qualified CPA to serve as an independent source of information.

Corporations should carry liability insurance covering activities of their members, even on errands for the organization. Volunteers are, in fact, "gratuitous employees" when they are performing under direction and supervision of organizational or agency officers. The extent of the corporate and individual liability should be clearly spelled out, and expectations of the Board members well defined.

The obligation to exercise due care means each director is liable for any losses the corporation may suffer through negligence, though not error in judgment, if the director can show he acted in good faith.

Of importance here is that each Board member be informed fully of his liability when accepting a position as Director with any corporation, even non-profit.

SUGGESTED READING

1. Voluntarism

Brown, Kathleen M, *Keys To Making a Volunteer Program Work,* Arden Publications, Richmond, CA, 1982

Davis, Maxine, *Get the Most Out of the Best Years,* Hadden Craftsmen, Pa., 1960

Do It Voluntarily, Junior League of San Diego, 1978

Fessler, Donald R., *Facilitating Community Change,* University Associates, La Jolla, Ca., 1976

Hanlon, Brenda, *The Best of Val,* The National Center For Citizen Involvement, Washington, DC, 1980

Flanagan, Joan, *The Successful Volunteer Organization,* Chicago Books, Inc., Chicago, 1981

I Can, American Red Cross, 1981

Lewis, C. O., Leo F. Johnson, *Keys to Creative Work With Volunteers,* Worcester, Mass.

Naylor, Harriet H., *Volunteers Today,* Dryden, N.Y., 1973

Scheitlin, George, and Eleanore L. Gillstrom, *Recruiting and Developing Volunteer Leaders,* Parish Life Press, Philadelphia PA 1973

Sochen, June, *Movers and Shakers,* Quadrangle/New York Times Book Co., N.Y., 1974

Stone, Julita Martinez, *How To Volunteer in Social Service Agencies,* Charles C. Thomas, Springfield, Ill., 1982

2. Meetings

Bradford, Leland P., *Making Meeting Work,* University Associates, LaJolla, Ca., 1976

Doyle, Michael, and David Straus, *How To Make Meetings Work,* Wyden, N.Y., 1976

Lawson, John D., *When You Preside,* Interstate Printers & Publishers, Danville, Ill., 1980

Schindler-Rinman, Eva, and Ronald Lippitt, *Taking Your Meetings Out of the Doldrums,* University Associates, La Jolla, Ca.

3. Board Skills

The Nonprofit Board in 1983, Voluntary Action Leadership, Arlington, Va., 1983

Nordhoff, Nancy S., et al. *Fundamental Practices for Success With Volunteer Boards for Non-Profit Organizations,* 1983

O'Connell, Brian, *Effective Leadership in Voluntary Organizations,* Follett Publishing, Chicago, Ill., 1976

Wilson, Marlene, *Effective Management of Volunteer Programs,* Volunteer Management Associates, Boulder, Colo., 1979

4. Group Process

Berne, E., *Games People Play,* Grove Press, N.Y., 1964

Bion, W.R., *Experiences in Groups,* Ballentine, N.Y., 1975

Bonner, Hubert, *The Group & Dynamics,* Ronald Press Co., N.Y., 1959

Egan, Gerald, *Encounter: Group Process for Interpersonal Growth,* Brooks/Cole Publishing Co., Belmont, Ca., 1970

5. Leadership

Beal, George M., Joe Bohlen & J. Neil Raudabaugh, *Leadership & Dynamic Group Action,* Iowa State University Press, Ames, Iowa, 1962

Burke, W. Warner, Interpersonal Communications, in William Lassey and Richard R. Fernandez, (Eds), *Leadership and Social Change,* University Associates, La Jolla, Ca., 1976

Hill, Napoleon, *Success Through A Positive Mental Attitude,* Prentice-Hall, Inc. N.Y., 10020

Lawson, Leslie Griffin, et al, *Lead On!,* Impact Publishers, San Luis Obispo, Ca., 1982

Uris, Auren, *How to be a Successful Leader,* McGraw-Hill, N.Y., 1953

6. Motivation

Anderson, Richard, *Motivation: The Master Key,* Correan Publications, Los Gatos, Ca., 1973

Buscaglia, Leo, *Love,* Fawcett Books, Brooklyn, N.Y., 1972

Carnegie, Dale, *How To Win Friends and Influence People,* Pocket Books, N.Y., 1936

Ford, Edward, and Robert Zorn, *Why Be Lonely,* Argus Communications, Niles, Ill., 1975

Glasser, W., *Reality Therapy,* Harper & Row, N.Y., 1965

Levin, Stanley, "How to Motivate Volunteers", *Volunteers in Rehabilitation,* Washington, D.C., Goodwill Industries of America, Inc., 1973 Booklet #9

Luthans, F., and R. Kreitner, *Organizational Behavior Modification,* Scott Forsman, Glenview, Ill., 1975

McClelland, D.C. (ED.), *Human Motivation,* General Learning Press, Morristown, N.J., 1973

Maslow, Abraham, *Motivation & Personality,* Harper and Row, N.Y., 1954

Pell, Arthur R., *Recruiting, Training & Motivating Volunteer Workers,* Pilot Books, N.Y., 1972

7. Communication

Erikson, Karin, *Communication Skills for Human Services,* Reston, Reston Publishing, 1979

Fast, Julius, *Body Language,* M. Evans & Co., Inc., c/o J.B. Lippincott, Philadelphia, Pa., 1970

Miller, Sherod, *Alive and Aware: Improving Communication in Relationships,* Minneapolis, Minn, 1975

Mortensen, D. David, *Communication, The Study of Interaction,* McGraw-Hill, N.Y., 1972

Fleishman, Alfred, *Troubled Talk,* International Society for General Semantics, San Francisco, Ca., 1973

8. Listening

Adler, Mortimer J., *How to Speak, How to Listen,* MacMillian, N.Y., 1983

Condon, John Jr., *Semantics and Communication,* MacMillian, N.Y., 1966

Erikson, Karin, *Communication Skills for Human Services,* Reston Publishing, Co., 1979

Faber, Adele, and Elaine Mazlish, *How to Talk so Kids will Listen and How to Listen so Kids will Talk,* Avon Books, N.Y., 1982

Hayakawa, S.I., *Language in Thought and Action,* Harcourt, Brace & World, N.Y., 1964

Reik, Theodore, *Listening With the Third Ear,* Pyramid, N.Y., 1968

9. Problem Solving

Adams, James, *Conceptual Blockbusting, A Guide To Better Ideas,* W.W. Norton & Co., Inc., N.Y., 1979

Anderson, H.H., *Creativity & Its Cultivation,* Harper & Row, 1959

deBono, Edward, *New Think,* N.Y. Basic Books, 1967

Huff, Darrell, *How To Lie With Statistics,* W. W. Norton & Co., Inc., N.Y., 1954

Kaufman, Roger, *Identifying and Solving Problems: A System Approach,*

Osborn, Alex, *Applied Imagination,* Scribner, N.Y., 1979

Maltz, Maxwell, *Psycho Cybernetics,* Prentice-Hall, N.Y., 1960

Patton, Bobby R., and Kim Giffin, *Problem Solving and Group Interaction,* Harper and Row, N.Y., 1973

Straus, David, *Participatory Decision Making,* AMACOM, N.Y., 1974

Tuckman, Bruce, *Conducting Educational Research,* Harcout, Brace, Jananovich, S.F., 1972

10. Time Management

Bliss, Edwin, *Getting Things Done,* the ABC's of Time Management

Ferner, Jack D., *Successful Time Management,* John Wiley and Sons, NN, N.Y., 1980

Hobbs, Charles R., "Insight on Time Management", Salt Lake City, Charles R. Hobbs Corp., 1978

Lakein, Alan, *How To Get Control of Your Time and Your Life,* Peter H. Wyden, Inc., N.Y., 1973

MacKenzie, R.A., *Managing Time at the Top,* The Presidents Association, N.Y., 1970

MacKenzie, R.A., *New Time Management Methods,* The Dartnell Corp., Chicago, Ill., 1975

11. Management By Objectives

Crosby, Philip B., *The Art of Getting Your Own Sweet Way,* McGraw Hill, N.Y., 1972

Hanson, Pauline, *The Board Member — Decision Maker for the Non-Profit Corporation,*

LeBoeuf, M., *Working Smart,* McGraw-Hill, N.Y., 1979

McConkey, Dale B., *How To Manage By Results,* 3rd ed., AMACOM, N.Y., 1977

O'Connell, Brian, *Effective Leadership in Voluntary Organizations,* Follett Publishing, Chicago, Ill., 1976

Peter, Laurence J., & Raymond Hull, *The Peter Principle,* Bantam, N.Y., 1969

Tosi, Henry L., and Jerald W. Young, *Management, Experiences and Demonstrations,* Richard D. Irwin, Inc., Homewood, Ill., 1980

Wilson, Marlene, *The Effective Management of Volunteer Programs,* Volunteer Management Associates, Boulder, Co., 1979

12. Conflict Management

Benne, Kenneth D., and Muntyan, Bozida, *Human Relations in Curriculum Change,* Dryden Press, N.Y., 1951

Cohen, Herb, *You Can Negotiate Anything,* Stuart, Secaucus, N.J., 1980

Hart, Lois B, *Learning from Conflict,* Addison-Wesley Publishing Co., Reading, MA, 1981

Kniveton, Broomley, *Training For Negotiating,* Business Books, London, 1978

Weisinger, Dr. Hendrie, and Lobsenz, Norman M., *Nobody's Perfect (How to Give Criticism and Get Results),* Warner Books, N.Y., N.Y., 1983

13. Self Assessment/Group Assessment

Campbell, David, *If You Don't Know Where You're Going You'll Probably End up Somewhere Else,* Argus Communications, Niles, Ill., 1974

Halas, Celia, and Roberta Matteson, *I've Done So Well, Why Do I Feel So Bad?* MacMillan, N.Y., 1977

Harragan, Lehan, *Games Mother Never Taught You,* Rawson Associates, N.Y., 1977

Howell, Mary C., *Helping Ourselves,* Beacon Press, Boston, 1975

Kiev, Ari, M.D., *A Strategy for Success,* MacMillan, N.Y., 1977

Kurtz, Paul, *Exuberance,* Prometheus Books, Buffalo, N.Y., 1977

Newman, Mildred, and Bernard Berkowitz, *How to Take Charge of Your Life,* Bantam, N.Y., 1978

Newman, Mildred, and Bernard Berkowitz, *How to be Your Own Best Friend,* Ballantine, N.Y., 1975

Rogers, Carl, *On Becoming a Person,* Houghton-Mifflin, Boston, Mass., 1961

Steiner, Claud M., *Scripts People Live: Transactional Analysis of Life Scripts*, Grove Press, N.Y., 1974

Weinberg, Dr. George, *Self Creation*, Avon, N.Y., 1978

14. Publicity

Delacorte, Toni, *How to Get Free Press*, G. P. Putman's Sons, S.F., Ca., 1981

Hall, Babette, *The Right Angles, How to Do Successful Publicity*, I. Washburn, N.Y., 1965

Kurtz, Harold, *Public Relations and Fund Raising for Hospitals*, Thomas, Springfield, Ill., 1981

15. Career Development

Bolles, Richard, *What Color Is Your Parachute?* Ten Speed Press, Berkeley, Ca., 1972

Eisen, Jeffrey, *Get The Right Job Now*, Lippincott, N.Y., 1978

Fader, Shirley, *From Kitchen to Career*, Stein and Day, N.Y., 1977

Jame, Muriel and Jongeward, Dorothy, *Born To Win*, Addison-Wesley Publishing, Reading, Mass., 1976

Haldane, Bernard, *Career Satisfaction and Success*, AMACOM, 1974

Lobb, Charlotte, *Exploring Careers Through Volunteerism*, Rosen, N.Y., 1976

Scholz, Nell Tumlin, Judith Sosebee Prince, Gordon Porter Miller, *How To Decide — A Workbook for Women*, Avon Books, 1975

INDEX